Studies in Buddhist Economics, Management, and Policy

Series Editors

Clair Brown
University of California, Berkeley
Berkeley, USA

László Zsolnai
Corvinus University Budapest
Budapest, Hungary

This book series is devoted to exploring and presenting new developments in contemplative inquiry related to Buddhist Economics, Well-Being, Social Transformation, Mindful Organizations, and Ecological Worldview in management and policy contexts. This particular combination of fields represents a unique nexus for reflection and action toward developing ways of mindful and sustainable management for organizations in the economic and social life.

More information about this series at
http://www.palgrave.com/gp/series/16318

Ernest C. H. Ng

Introduction to Buddhist Economics

The Relevance of Buddhist Values in Contemporary Economy and Society

palgrave
macmillan

Ernest C. H. Ng
Centre of Buddhist Studies
The University of Hong Kong
Hong Kong, People's Republic of China

Studies in Buddhist Economics, Management, and Policy
ISBN 978-3-030-35113-7   ISBN 978-3-030-35114-4 (eBook)
https://doi.org/10.1007/978-3-030-35114-4

This Palgrave Macmillan imprint is published by the registered company Springer Nature Switzerland AG.
The registered company address is: Gewerbestrasse 11, 6330 Cham, Switzerland

This book is dedicated to my teachers, friends and family members for their compassion and wisdom; and to all colleagues at the Centre of Buddhist Studies, The University of Hong Kong and European SPES Institute for their dedication to the teaching and research on Buddhist Studies and spirituality in economics and society; and to László Zsolnai and Clair Brown for their mentorship and leadership in the field of Buddhist Economics.

Preface

Living in a market-driven economy where short-term profit and economic growth appear to be the ultimate goal, this book aims to explore how Buddhist teachings could bridge the divide between our spiritual and material needs and reconcile the tension between doing good for social interest and doing well for financial success. It also attempts to serve as a pioneering effort to systematically introduce Buddhist Economics as an interdisciplinary subject to audience with limited background in the field of either Buddhism or economics.

Having spent over fifteen years in the financial sector as an investment banker and an asset manager, I witnessed two financial crises firsthand—the first being the Asian Financial Crisis of 1997 and the second being the Global Financial Crisis of 2007–2008. Financial capital is a boon in the desert, but the drowning man curses it. The risks and returns of financial volatilities can mean great fortunes for some but also great havoc for others. Experiencing these financial crises made me wonder: what are the Buddhist responses to the ups and downs in the market? If the *Buddha* offers great inspiration for those going through the unavoidable ups and downs of life, what insights do his teachings offer for those engaging with the ups and downs of the market economy? After all, both the markets and life can also be described as dreams and bubbles. In a profit-driven market economy, conflicts between the pursuit of profit and non-profit values seem to be unavoidable—a constant struggle between doing good and doing well (Fig. 1). Can we live in a market economy and achieve sustainable development consistent with Buddhist values? Can Buddhist teachings contribute to a sustainable economy?

Fig. 1 Path to the Tigers Nest in Bhutan. Note: Path to the Tigers Nest in Paro, Bhutan. (Source: Photo by author)

These questions motivate me to embark upon a long and fruitful journey of research, learning and teaching, joining a growing network of scholars and experts in the field of Buddhist Economics from different parts of the world. I have the privilege to have László Zsolnai at Corvinus University of Budapest as my PhD external examiner and mentor. Together with his colleagues such as Gábor Kovács, Knut Ims, and Hendrik Opdebeeck at the Community of the European Management Schools (CMES) and the European SPES (spirituality in economics and society) Institute, he has assembled a reputable group of scholars and professionals focusing on the interdisciplinary studies of spirituality, ethics, values in business, and economic activities. Zsolnai has been engaged in the field of Buddhist Economics for more than 25 years and has built a strong research base connecting different fields in Europe. In 2017, Clair Brown at the University of California, Berkeley launched her seminal work *Buddhist Economics* in the United States. Like Zsolnai, Brown is well-recognized as a scholar in the traditional school of economics but has also realized the necessity of moving beyond the traditional paradigms. Brown has been teaching an undergraduate seminar on Buddhist Economics, which she believes to be "a framework that integrates global sustainability and shared prosperity along with care for the human spirit."

Zsolnai and Brown together form a global network of academic and professional experts looking into the field of Buddhist Economics from the perspective of sectoral, doctrinal, and textual studies; philosophical and metaphysical analyses; and applicational and contemporary explorations. The *Palgrave Studies in Buddhist Economics Series* is an important milestone they lead to highlight the latest research in the field. I am grateful that this book could contribute to the series by leveraging my teaching experience from the Buddhism and Economics undergraduate course at the University of Hong Kong with over 150 students each year since 2017. It is our hope that this book could serve a growing body of students who may benefit from learning this subject.

This book is the dependent-arising of all the wisdom and efforts of all scholars in the past and present—and hopefully leading to further research in the future. It was also a valuable manifestation of the true spirit of Buddhist Economics, which involves non-instrumental uses, genuine care, and generosity. I am particularly grateful of Zsolnai and Brown who are truly generous, caring, and humble about sharing their expertise with others. Throughout their celebrated careers, their successes have also contributed to the successes of their peers and successors. They aspire others to build a global network that can enable economics to bring real benefit to mankind. It is nonetheless critical to continue to make the subject more relevant to a broader audience and put Buddhist Economics into actions. As Brown advocated: "To embrace and practice Buddhist economics, you need courage to change, courage to protect the environment, courage to promote justice, and courage to live with joy."

Hong Kong, People's Republic of China Ernest C. H. Ng

Acknowledgements

I thank everyone at Palgrave who have encouraged and worked with me to get this book into print over the last couple of years, but especially Ms. Elizabeth Graber. I also thank Ms. Sophia Siegler and Mr. Vipin Kumar Mani for their very important editorial assistance and Mr. Samuel Wong for his advice on Buddhist terms in Pāli and Sanskrit at a crucial time.

Contents

Abbreviations

AN	*Aṅguttara Nikāya*, the "numerical" discourses
CDB	*The Connected Discourses of the Buddha* (translation of SN; see Bodhi (2000a))
Dhp	Dhammapada
DN	*Dīgha Nikāya*, the "long" discourses
LDB	*The Long Discourses of the Buddha* (translation of DN; see Walshe (1986))
MLDB	*The Middle Length Discourses of the Buddha* (translation of MN; see Ñanamoli and Bodhi (1995))
MN	*Majjhima Nikāya*, the "middle-length" discourses
NDB	*The Numerical Discourse* (translation of AN; see Bodhi (2012))
Skt	Sanskrit
SN	*Saṃyutta Nikāya*, the "connected" discourses
Sn	Sutta Nipāta
Ud	*Khuddaka Nikāya*, the collection of little texts

List of Figures

List of Tables

List of Boxes

Introduction

This book is a pioneering effort to systematically introduce Buddhist Economics as an interdisciplinary subject at the fundamental level to audience with limited background in the field of either Buddhism or economics. It elaborates some core concepts in Buddhist teachings, their relevancy to economy and society, and means of achieving sustainability for individuals, society and the environment through the cultivation of ethical living and well-being. It is also unique in its attempt to bridge traditional spiritual theories with contemporary applications, showcasing the great potential of the Buddhist and spirituality perspectives for reinventing economics and business practices.

Through contemporary scholarly research and case studies from a wide range of relevant fields including Buddhist studies, economics, behavioral finance, cognitive science, and psychology, the book illustrates the relevance and efficacy of Buddhist values for ethical and sustainable decision-making in the contemporary economy and society.

This book is most relevant to students and academics of interdisciplinary studies such as Buddhist Economics, Spirituality in Economics and Society, Sustainable Finance, Social Entrepreneurship, and Impact Investing. It could serve as the primary textbook for undergraduate and postgraduate students in Buddhist Economics and related subjects.

PART I

The Subject and Framework

CHAPTER 1

What Is Buddhist Economics?

Buddhism: The Teacher, the Teachings, and Students

The word "*Buddha*" is not a name but a title designated to "one who has woken up." It refers to an extremely rare and extraordinary class of beings that have awakened to the "knowledge of the world as it truly is and in so doing finds release from suffering" (Gethin 1998). The *Buddha* is a man, but an extraordinary one. He is not a savior but a teacher (*satthar* as frequently appeared in the ancient *Pāli* texts). Realizing the true nature of sufferings, he teaches out of compassion and sympathy the path of the cessation of suffering for the benefit and welfare of all living things. With his teachings, the *Buddha* set in motion the wheel of *dhamma* and established a community of disciples, the *saṅgha*.

Despite his profound wisdom in discovering and delivering the path to enlightenment to others, the Buddha is not a god. He is more of a super spiritual being who has achieved enlightenment in his life time as a human being, a living example of how ordinary human beings could eventually achieve the extraordinary through many life-times of excelling the practice of compassion and wisdom. He is therefore respected and honored for his achievements and teachings.

There are other gods in Buddhism representing higher planes of existence, but they are also being bound by the same laws of cause and effect, just as there are also other lower realms of existence. The *Buddha* or those achieve enlightenments have transcended above the cycles of birth and

E. C. H. Ng, *Introduction to Buddhist Economics*,
Studies in Buddhist Economics, Management, and Policy,
https://doi.org/10.1007/978-3-030-35114-4_1

death and conditioned sufferings through enlightenment. Other enlightened followers share the same traits, but a *Buddha* has the profound wisdom and compassion required to lead others towards the path of spiritual learning and their own realization.

Tracing the historical evidences of the *Buddha* is a difficult task. There were no biographies or written documents from his era, and the earliest were rooted in remarks reportedly made by the *Buddha* when he taught drawing from his own experiences. Later Buddhist sources usually focus on the *Buddha*'s quest towards enlightenment in relation to his teachings, highlighting Buddhist doctrines. These remarks were verbal transmission initially until they are formally transcribed in the written forms. The earliest sources on the *Buddha*'s life story are the "*Pāli* canonical 'discourses' of the *Buddha*, the *suttas* and texts on monastic discipline, the *vinaya*" (Cantwell 2010). Initially Buddhist philosophies were developed alongside other Indian religions, adopting and reinterpreting some of their concepts and practices. The rich mythology and complex monastic codes were later adoptions. One mythical account states the moment the *Buddha* was born, he stood upright, walked seven steps and confirmed this would be his final birth (i.e. no future rebirth). *Buddha*-s come into the world when it is mature enough for their presence, achieve enlightenment, teach and then enter into final liberation.

Box 1.1 The *Buddha, Dhamma,* and the *Saṅgha*

The *Buddha*, *dhamma*, and the *saṅgha* are together the "three jewels" (*tiratana*) which are the most valuable and reliable treasures for us to take refuge in.

As stated in the *Vatthūpama Sutta* (MLDB. MN 7), the *Buddha*, the Blessed One, is "accomplished, fully enlightened, perfect in true knowledge and conduct, sublime, knower of the worlds, incomparable leader of persons to be tamed, teacher of gods and humans, enlightened, blessed."

The *dhamma*, is "well proclaimed by the Blessed One, visible here and now, immediate effective, inviting inspection, onward leading, to be experienced by the wise for themselves."

The *saṅgha*, is "practicing the good way, practicing the straight way, practicing the true way, practicing the proper way, that is, the four pairs of persons, the eight types of individuals; [it] is worthy of gifts, worthy of hospitality, worthy of offerings, worthy of reverential salutation, the unsurpassed field of merit for the world".

The historical *Buddha*, the one we currently look into, lived in *Kapilavatthu* on what is currently the Indian-Nepalese border. He was born as *Siddhattha Gotama* of the clan of *Sakya*. The earliest Buddhist sources, dated from the fourth or third century BCE, additionally mentioned he was the son of a local chieftain *rājan*. Later Buddhist accounts may tend to exaggerate the wealth of the *Buddha*, making him out to be a royal prince as opposed to a member of an important aristocrat family. Nonetheless, he lived a comfortable, luxurious life. From birth, he had been prophesized to either be a great 'wheel-turning' king (Pāli: *cakkavattin*) or a *Buddha*, and his father tried to his best to ensure *Siddhattha* was sheltered from the ugliness of the world. But one day, leaving his palace, he encountered a withered old man, a sick man, and a corpse being carried to the funeral. He realized that his life is also subject to suffering in the form of sickness, old age, and death like everyone else anyway, mundane pleasures are not solid and worthy. Upon spotting a peaceful wandering ascetic who illustrated the possibility of practice and training, he decided to leave home and follow the footsteps of all noble practitioners. This tradition is sometimes known as the "renouncer (Skt.: *saṁnyāsin*) tradition." Basically, it refers to individuals who renounce "their normal role in society as a member of an extended 'household' in order to devote themselves to some form of religious or spiritual life" (Gethin 1998). The renouncer tradition often includes undertaking austerities (fasting, enduring extreme weathers and physical discomfort, etc.), cultivating meditative techniques to obtain a deeper understanding of the world, and forming philosophical views to support particular practices and the knowledge they have gained from them. They depend on alms to sustain their livelihood.

The *Samaṇas* (Pāli) preached a very frugal code of conduct as well as offered space for spiritual and philosophical experimentation. Anyone was welcome to join regardless of their social background. Buddhist monastic order represented a "Middle Way" between the hermit *Samaṇas* life and the householder life. It emphasized monastics as a community with close relations to its lay patrons. By the fifth century BCE, the tradition had become quite widespread.

Siddhattha studied under various teachers, engaging in severe austerities before realizing the futility of such practices. The *Mahāsaccaka Sutta* notes that extreme ascetic practices made his body too weak to properly meditate and could not possibly be the path to enlightenment (MLDB. MN 36). The recognition came with a recollection of a meditative experience he had had as a child. He had been sitting in the cool shade of a rose-apple tree and entered "a state of focused rapture" (Cantwell 2010) that was absent of all unwholesome thoughts. Concluding it was the foundation for enlightenment, and combined with the strength and mental clarity gained from eating again, the *Buddha* finally achieved awakening. The contrast between his luxurious palace life and his ascetic lifestyle further emphasized the Buddhist idea of the Middle Way.

According to the *Pāli sutta* text, the *Buddha* first focused his mind and banished all sensual and evil thoughts. That was the first deep absorption. He entered the second and third through further concentration, and successfully purified his mental equanimity in the fourth deep absorption. His mind had become "focused, undisturbed, pure and free from defilement" (Cantwell 2010). From there, in the first watch of the night, he was able to freely revisit his past lives and fully comprehend the cycle of life and death. The second watch enlightened him to the knowledge that one's actions affected which state they would be reborn in. The third watch directed him towards the destruction of craving. Through understanding how craving arose, he was able to put a stop to it. Ignorance dispelled, he escaped the cycle of rebirth. The *Buddhacarita* version includes a fourth watch in which the *Buddha* attained the state of omniscience.

He finally gained enlightenment while meditating under an *assattha* tree near the *Nairañjarā* in what is now known as the north Indian state of *Bihar*. The *sutta* mentioned that once the *Buddha* had conceptualized his path to enlightenment, he dropped his alms bowl in the *Nerañjara* River and asked it travel against the current if he was right. Miraculously, the bowl was swept upstream. While impossible to comprehend what he truly experienced, the *sutta* refers it to "bodhi" or "awakening" and involving the deepest understanding of the insight into the doctrine of dependent arising and the Four Noble Truths, being the nature of suffering, its cause, its cessation, and the way leading to its cessation (Gethin 1998). While anyone can achieve enlightenment, some may not want to. An analogy likens the *Buddha* to a doctor with a cure, but it is up to the patient take the medicine. As mentioned in the early *Ariyapariyesanā Sutta* (MLDB. MN 26), the *Buddha* reflects his discoveries go against most people's understanding. His discoveries and teachings, the *dhamma* is what even "the [*Buddha*] found hard to reach. For it will never be perceived by those who live in lust and hate."

The *Buddha* spent the rest of his life teaching the way to the cessation of suffering. The Dharma Wheel, often placed above the entrances of Buddhist temples, symbolizes Buddhist teachings' ability to replace and cease the endless cycle of suffering (Fig. 1.1). The Wheel is typically flanked by two deer, representative of the ones found in the game park in *Sarnath.* The Wheel has eight spokes to symbolize the eight aspects of the Noble Eightfold Path, which are meant to work together instead of in sequence. He is said to have advised the rulers of his time on successful government and spiritual well-being as well, going against specified role models in Brahmanical texts. He had amassed a respectable community of disciples, the *saṅgha*, who refrain from household life.

Fig. 1.1 The *Buddha*. Note: A bronze statue of *Buddha* setting the *dhamma*-wheel in motion. (Source: Photo by author)

Box 1.2 Twelve Acts in the Life of the *Buddha*

Tibetan sources further split the *Buddha*'s life into twelve acts that are performed by all *Buddha*-s. *Theravādin* texts are even longer with thirty features that are the rule (Pāli: *dhammatā*) for all *Buddha*-s.

The first of twelve acts is living in heaven, as the result of having practiced "the perfections" (Pāli: *pāramī*) over numerous lifetimes. The second and third acts are intertwined; the *Buddha* was conceived during a full moon in July and that night, his mother *Mahāmāyā* (Pāli) dreamt that a white elephant carrying a white lotus in its trunk entered her womb. When the Bodhisattva was born, he walked "seven steps to the north and proclaimed, 'I am chief in the world, I am best in the world, I am first in the world. This is my last birth. There will be no further rebirth.'" (Gethin 1998) That was the fourth act. Sources state *Siddhattha* had a wife and son, *Yaśodharā* and *Rāhula*—the fifth act which points to "Bodhisattva's enjoyment of proficiency in worldly skills and sensuality." (Gethin 1998) Disillusionment with his privileged life marked the sixth act. The seventh was his leaving home, the "great going forth" (Pāli: *mahāpabbajjā*), which also took place on a full moon.

The *Buddha* was 29 when he became a wandering ascetic. His grueling six-year practice of severe austerities became the eighth act. Realizing the uselessness of tormenting his body, he accepted an offering of milk-rice from a young woman named *Sujāta* (Pāli) (or *Nandabalā* in some accounts) to nourish himself and sat under an *assattha* tree to meditate.

The tree is now dubbed the Bodhi tree or tree of awakening, for it is where *Siddhattha* became a *Buddha*. He then lifted his right hand and touched the ground, calling on the very earth to be his witness. Incidentally, it is the very pose most statues of the *Buddha* depict. The ninth and tenth acts had been obtained; he had defeated Mara and attained complete awakening.

The *Buddha* then went to the five companions that had accompanied him during his period of severe austerities and showed them the path to the cessation of suffering. Such is the eleventh act: "setting in motion" or "turning the wheel of *dhamma*" (Pāli: *dhammacakkappavattana*). He taught for forty-five years, as one of the six *arahant*-s that would arrive in this world. His death completed the twelfth and last act—"full going out" (Pāli: *parinibbāna*). All things are impermanent and unreliable, and the *Buddha* is no exception.

Market Economy: Core Components and Mechanics of the Machine

While economics as a subject is further analyzed in Chap. 3, it is important to note that the subject is an evolving one with many different schools of thought based upon a wide range of assumptions and theories about human behaviors and the world. Market economy in this book refers to a wide range of economic systems, from the free market economy to socialist democracy, which rely heavily on the market operations in transactions, price-discovery, and resource allocation. As discussed by Ng (2015) and Chang (2014), it is challenging to categorize an operating economic system only with one definite school of economic thought. Yet market economy should share the core characteristics and assumptions of Classical and Neoclassical schools based on rationality and self-interest, profit maximization, materialism, and even more with the Neoclassical school's reliant on the dominant role of the market exchange and consumption. Market economy may not be entirely "free" from government and other forces of intervention, but in terms of its reliance on government, it is on the "right side" of the spectrum in opposite directions with Keynesian, Developmentalist or even the Marxist on the "left".

To explain the mechanics of the market economic machine, scholars over centuries have attempted to offer theories which integrate the microeconomics at the individual level and the macroeconomic at the societal level. Yet it is even more demanding to describe this integration in day-to-day market activities through a simple model. In *How the Economic Machine Works*, Dalio (2015)[1] attempts to offer a clear and succinct explanation of how the economy works by connecting both the microeconomic and the macroeconomic theory. In his view, an economy is simply "the sum of the transactions that make it up." The market consists of buyers and sellers conducting transactions. A transaction means a buyer gives money or credit to a seller in exchange for a good, a service, or a financial asset. Different buyers and sellers have different motivations. One can trace these motivations and use them to understand the economy. This perspective of supply and demand differs from the traditional one, where both

[1] Ray Dalio is the founder, president and co-chief investment officer of Bridgewater Associates, one of the largest hedge funds in the world. As of Dec. 2019, Bridgewater Associates managed approximately US$160 billion and received over 50 industry awards and various recognitions in the past 10 years.

supply and demand are measured in quantity and the price relationship between them is linked to elasticity. Instead it focuses on factors typically ignored, such as the amount of money spent (in contrast to quantity bought), who spent it (distinguishing between individual buyers and their motivations), and why they did so. The market fluctuates according to these factors and neglecting them creates a theoretical and inaccurate view of the market and economy.

Wealth could be created through an increase in money earned from today's productivity, but also across time horizon through the creation of credit. Credit is created when one's present wealth is lent out in exchange for a loan or a promise to be repaid with the other's wealth (Dalio 2015). Most spending nowadays stems from credit creation and does not require money to go around to work. Credit can technically be created from thin air (though subject to central bank policies); as long as both parties are willing, a transaction can be made solely through credit.

In a market-based system, transactions occur through free will, that is, buyers and sellers act in pursuit of their own interests. Supply and demand of wealth over goods determined the price of a particular goods (Dalio 2015). Similarly, the price (or interest rate) of the credit created is determined by the supply and demand of wealth today over wealth tomorrow, with consideration to the probability of repayment, i.e. the borrowers' creditworthiness. Though we may have different views on the price of money today over tomorrow, creditors would be willing to lower the interest rate for borrowers of higher creditworthiness if the risk of non-repayment is low.

Credit could be constructive either in the form of consumption today or in the form of investment, which could be more than repaid by an increase in productivity tomorrow. Without credit, one can only spend or invest in what one can earn today even though such spending could generate even higher return tomorrow. The increase in economic activities and wealth through the creation of credit can increase one's creditworthiness and create a virtuous cycle if productivity can be sustained. Otherwise, it could create a vicious cycle where one spends more than one can repay in the future. In the process, creditworthiness is reduced, and wealth is destroyed when creditors cannot get their money back in full. In bubbles, the amount of credit outweighs what can be paid back and leads to busts.

The combination of psychology and credit can provide insight into countries' economic life cycles. Money and credit can be invested to create sufficient returns to pay debts and finance more growth. However, as countries grow wealthier, credit created tends to fuel consumption as opposed to investment. A decrease in investment for worthwhile projects results in slower productivity growth, even as the borrowing and spending raises income and makes labor more expensive.

Human nature (cultured and nutured) also plays a large part in governing people's productivity and indebtedness. The desire for higher living standards motivates people to work harder until their earnings near equilibrium levels. In short, levels of productivity and indebtedness change in relation to income growth. Economic conditions affect human nature, and vice versa. Economic life cycles evolve so gradually—over at least a century—most people, central bankers or policy markers do not notice. Hence, these cycles are not controlled, which is why they are destined to appear. If human nature were different, so that debt growth would not overtake income growth and income growth would not overtake productivity growth, these cycles would rarely exist.

According to Dalio (2015), the macro economy works like a machine, aggregating the productivity, wealth (money and credit) and goods available in the entire society. He observes that government has a critical role in the economic machine—both in the form of central government and central bank. The central government has the unique fiscal function and authority to create jobs through fiscal spending, redistribute wealth through taxation on wealth and subsidies for the low-income. On the other hand, the central bank can increase credit supply either through the creation or the destruction of credit by reducing or increasing money supply respectively; or increase the money supply by printing money—typical through purchasing bonds or even outright "printing" money. The central bank can also determine foreign exchange rates to adjust the worth of one country's currency relative to others to alter the terms of trade *vis-à-vis* other countries.

There are five important features in Dalio's analysis on how the economic machine works. First of all, the government has a critical role in its fiscal and monetary capacity. The market may be the invisible hand that guides economic activities, but the government has, time and time again, affected the economic cycle regarding wealth creation and destruction. Second, while productivity has a rather linear relationship with wealth creation over time, wealth is created or destroyed in the short-term through the credit cycle, and in the long-term through the leverage cycle of a bigger scale. When society borrows beyond its future productivity, there is more wealth available in the short-term, driving asset prices up. This process, however, creates an illusion that the value of collateral behind credit increases and hence, the borrower becomes more creditworthy to sustain existing or even more investment. This will further drive the cost of credit lower and increase demand for leverage. Hence, an exuberating leverage bubble is created to a tipping point where a fall in price will trigger a vicious downward cycle which most often ends in an avalanche-style panicky collapse.

A responsible central bank might have prevented crises from happening in advance by reducing the availability of credit through increasing interest rates or reducing money supply through bond purchase, thus draining excess liquidity from the system. Failing that, a complete meltdown of the financial system like the Global Financial Crisis in 2008, may only be resuscitated by maintaining a very low interest rate and an easy monetary environment. Meanwhile, a government also needs to offer direct social support through jobless claims or by creating jobs through increasing government spending. This support will lead to a long deleveraging process, but since economic activities can be restored in a relatively short period, Dalio (2015) called it a "beautiful deleveraging." If an economy does not respond to stimulus policies, prices and productivity may remain low for a long period in a deflationary economy. In other scenarios where a government fails to maintain its creditworthiness, credit or money creation will fail, leading to hyperinflation and a currency crisis which could severely reduce the government's legitimacy. This may lead to the downfall of the government through massive social unrest or, in some extreme cases, riots and revolution.

The third important feature of Dalio's economic discussion is that economic principles should be empirical in nature. His approaches lay out possible scenarios under different circumstances without necessarily predicting or offering a definite outcome. It discusses the mechanics of the markets based on empirical evidence and observations of the past, leaving room for different interpretations in the future when circumstances or causal relationships change. It puts an important emphasis on the interaction between the decisions and actions of the key players involved. Fourthly, it embraces the co-arising and transformative nature of economic activities, realizing that there are at least two sides to a transaction resembling a double-entry of the accounting system: an expense for one is an income for another, a borrowing (liability) is also a loan (asset), and a spending today is a liability tomorrow, or an investment today is a return tomorrow. Finally, Dalio does not attempt to second guess or discuss the motivation behind an economic decision or why people pursue certain things and avoid others.

Buddhist Economics as a Subject

While Buddhist Economics as a field of research may still be new to many, it has received increasing research focus over the last few decades. The term Buddhist Economics is believed to have been coined by E. F. Schumacher in his pioneering work *Small is Beautiful* in the 1970s. Over the last few decades, scholars have responded and contributed to this interdisciplinary exchange between economics and Buddhism. This exchange led to a new field of study called Buddhist Economics which may be broadly divided into five approaches. To demonstrate the relevance of Buddhist values in contemporary economy and society, this book focuses on the fourth and fifth approaches. The following broadly outlines five different approaches on Buddhist Economics as a subject:

1. Canonical review;
2. Alternative visions and paths;
3. Analyses on the economic arrangements of Buddhist related institutions
4. Comparative study—to offer Buddhist interpretations and meanings of modern economic theory and definitions; and
5. Practical strategic models to contextualize and integrate Buddhist teachings into the market economy.

Canonical Review

The first approach reviews how economic subjects, as part of people's daily life, are discussed in ancient Buddhist texts without introducing an independent or comprehensive economic theory. This discussion can be dated back to the time of the *Buddha* with rich references from *Pāli* literature. Since human activities and motives are involved in all aspects of economic activities, the *Buddha* was primarily focused on the ethical aspect of the economy. His mission had nothing to do with the formulation of a comprehensive economic theory or introducing changes to the economic system. Since the primary focus of Buddhist teachings is our "moral, ethical and spiritual" developments, economic activities should be conducted and assessed on their contributions to moral developments (Nanayakkara 1995). This focus is a significant contrast with a market economy. In *An Introduction to Buddhist Ethics*, Harvey (2000) explored the subject from an ethical perspective and offered an elaborate overview of the ethical implications of economic activities as discussed by the *Buddha* and other Buddhist texts. *Buddha* discusses the topic of lay economic ethics, right livelihood, the moral and spiritual qualities leading to worldly success, the appropriate use of income, the Buddhist attitude to wealth, and so forth.

Rahula (2008) also contributed to this research approach by discussing the teachings of the *Buddha* on gaining wealth, retaining wealth, happiness, and decision-making in the *Pāli* texts. Hettiarachchi (2001) reviewed the key concepts in Buddhist Economics in the *Pāli Tipiṭaka*. His study offers a comprehensive review of early Buddhist positions in not only the fundamental concepts of Buddhism but also macro issues relating to social structure and the actions of both individuals and state-based economic planning. Abeynayake (2016) reminds us that the invaluable teachings of the *Buddha* in the social and economic dimension have a long history. These scholars demonstrate that the Buddhist teachings are inseparable from socio-economic welfare and human well-being—the happiness of this life and future existences, from the perspective of both materiality and spirituality. From this perspective, Buddhist Economics means Buddhist moral, ethical and spiritual guidelines for whatever the prevailing mode of socio-economic activities. The compilations of *Pāli* texts in Buddhist Economics above are comprehensive although without much reference to their application in the current market economy.

Alternative Visions and Paths

Buddhist Economics as an independent research topic was believed to be first presented in Schumacher's *Small is Beautiful* (1984). His approach offers an alternative non-material visions and paths to the existing market economic system. As a pioneer in this field, Schumacher is not a Buddhist, but a well-recognized economist who once worked with John Maynard Keynes in the macroeconomic studies. Schumacher delivered some landmark perspectives on development economics based on Buddhist values which were very different from the mainstream economic theories of his time. He believed that the economy should serve society "as if people mattered." On production, he echoed the Buddhist focus on right livelihood, because the human character is built and developed through work. Civilization is developed by building upon the progress or purification of human characters instead of the proliferation of desires.

Schumacher (1984) posits that Buddhist Economics emphasizes the role of humans. Each individual, as a member of society and part of the environment, should be treated as a human instead of simply serving as part of the economic machine. The economy should serve people and the environment. Technology should not undermine our engagement in work and creativity. Without wisdom, science and technology would only mean a greater concentration of economic power and violence against the environment. He suggested that production methods and equipment should be cheap enough to be widely accessible, suitable for small-scale operation and compatible with man's need for creativity. While modern economics equates the standard of living to the level of consumption and hence, leads to waste and exploitation of natural resources now and in the future, Buddhist Economics aspires to achieve maximum well-being with minimum consumption. Schumacher's vision for Buddhist Economics is a set of principles leading to a simplistic and non-violent life.

However, Zadek concerned whether this "small-scale" notion of Buddhist Economics proposed by Schumacher would be "divorced from" (1993) or "restricted to a denial" (1997) of the modern industrial economy. It could be a utopian vision because it offered a set of solutions to the problems without "any clear sense of *how* these changes were to come about" (1997). He criticized that the Intermediate Technology Development Group, which was built upon Schumacher's ideals, could not achieve real sustainability amidst the challenge of the market economy.[2]

Weber (1978) examined Buddhism even more critically. He concluded that Buddhist ethics is the "most world-rejecting." It constrains economic progress because it considers "all rational purposive activity as leading away from salvation [which is achievable] for only a few, even of those who have resolved [to] live in poverty, chastity, and unemployment." It has "no motivation toward a rational system for the methodical control of life. [It] accepted this world as eternally given…there was no development toward modern capitalism … Above all, there evolved no 'capitalist spirit,' …".

[2] Intermediate Technology Development Group is a British non-government organization founded by Schumacher with the aim of implementing his vision on an economics as if people mattered. Since 1960s, it has operated in the southern continents to develop small enterprises based on ethical and environmental sustainable principles using small-scale technology managed and owned by small local communities. Zadek (1997) challenged the resilience and meaning of some of the observed practices arising from the work of these organizations.

Hwang (2015) argues that Weber arrived at such a conclusion because Weber compared "the economic ethics of world religions," only with "the sociological method of ideal type…while ignoring their historical progress" of theses world religions. Hwang (2015) suggests that "[Weber] was interested in Asian religions only because they could be used as points of comparisons for studying the development of Western religion. Therefore, many crucial events in the history of Eastern religions had been neglected." In fact, Zadek (1997) posits that Schumacher's approach is closely related to Weber. Both of them seemed to imply that Buddhism is not consistent with economic growth: "What Weber saw as the restrictive and embedded social structures of Buddhism, Schumacher saw as the potential for an invigorated human economics. The quintessential sociologist meets the unequivocal utopian."

Studies by Puntasen (2008) on Buddhist Economics leads to a view that *paññā* should be the core mode of production—*paññā*-ism. In order to achieve sustainable happiness, all economic activities including production, consumption, and distribution should "have the ultimate goal to achieve sustainable *sukha* through *paññā*" (Puntasen 2007a). In the same line of thought, Chang (2006) aspires for a Wisdom-based Economy, as opposed to a knowledge-based economy, that "utilizes the totality of human wisdom in solving the entire spectrum of human economic problems to ensure the achievement of highest human happiness." In particular, he believes that a Wisdom-based Economy could: (1) present a comprehensive understanding of reality by bringing together fragmented, complex knowledge from all aspects of life; and (2) focus not on maximizing economic production or consumption but the real objective of maximizing utility or happiness for each fixed unit of goods and services involved. Economic growth is measured by the number of people and the degree of enlightenment per person.

These views on Buddhist Economics criticize the modern economic focus on material wealth and attempt to substitute the pursuit of material economic growth with *paññā*, or redefine the pursuit of wealth from the material to the spiritual one. Another example in a similar vein is the *Santi Asoke* Buddhist Reform Movement in Thailand which focuses on detachment from material desire and the development of spiritual freedom. It is very critical to the existing market economy—particularly the greed, competition and exploitation of market economy. The *Santi Asoke* Movement is also more progressive on social and environmental ethics (Essen 2010). Similarly, Magnuson (2011) attempts to offer a solution to the free market economy through an alternative Mindful Economics, while Sivaraksa (2011) offers important Buddhist teachings for the path for inner spiritual growth based on Buddhist philosophy.

These perspectives of Buddhist Economics, which highlight the instrumental function of material well-being and focus on an alternative non-material visions and paths of well-being, will resonate with Buddhists who share a similar ultimate goal. They may, however, appear to be irrelevant to those still engage in the pursuit of material well-being or focus on the maximizing appeal of market economy. If we adopt Buddhist Economics, which advocates simplicity and minimizing, does it mean a stop to progress or, even worse, deteriorating into a backward mode of economy and poverty?

Pryor (1991) was also concerned if Buddhist Economics would mean a simple, self-contained economy without a scale, or if we could successfully extrapolate our understanding of Buddhist teachings to meet our new challenges today. Considering that both positions could be equally well-argued and interpreted from Buddhist canonical texts, he advocates an economic system that takes the "middle path" between the left (socialist) and the right (market-based) in income distribution and the view of government intervention. While proposing a vision of economics supported by Buddhist values, Zadek (1997) argues that a Buddhist Economics needs "an adequate route map for bringing much-needed changes" and ensuring continuous progress and prosperity.

Analysis of the Economic Arrangements of Buddhist Related Institutions

The third approach to Buddhist Economics comprises discussions on the economic arrangements within the Buddhist *saṅgha*, institution or society, and the interaction between the institutions of the laity and *saṅgha* communities—economics of the monastics or religion in general (Harvey 2000). Daniels (2005) suggested this subfield called "economics of religion" which applied "traditional analyses of consumers, firms and institutions" to "religious organizations and behavior so that religious phenomena are seen as products of *homo economicus*." Reynolds and Clifford (1980) and Pryor (1991) contributed to this field by analyzing the relationship and tension between the monks and laity. Reynolds and Clifford (1980) explained that while the monastics are practitioners of the *dhamma* through committing to pure and selfless actions, they are economically dependent on the laity. The laity is the economically productive group supporting the monastics, creating prosperity through their virtuous acts of donations.

Appropriate *dhammic* interactions between the monastics and the laity were believed to contribute inevitably to the material and spiritual growth of the community—"As a result of the monk's pure and selfless actions, the laity prosper…The monks for their part, offer themselves selflessly to the pure *dhamma* and, as a result, the *dhamma* of world order flourishes thereby enabling the laity to continue to support the monk in their ascetic and renunciative endeavor" Reynolds and Clifford (1980).

Similarly, Pryor (1991) believes that economic growth is achieved through the collective impact of virtuous actions of individuals following the *dhamma*. This collective virtuous force could be understood as a positive externality or Leibenstein's concept of X-efficiency. One conclusion he draws from this understanding is the trade-off between monastics and the laity or a "complementarity between the *nibbanic* and the *kammic* strands of Buddhism. For *nibbana* to be achieved by some, the others must exist as well."

Zadek (1997) asserts that these relationships evolve over time and do not necessarily reflect "a mechanical enforcement of a set of guiding principles taught in the canonical texts." In fact, they reflect how Buddhist principles are understood and practiced in real life to allow for and accustom to "the needs of livelihood, institutional imperatives, and actions oriented towards inner transformation." Conclusions drawn from a monastic economy could also be limited regarding application and significance in situations where such a *saṅgha* and laity institution is well-established.

Daniels (1998) also contributes to this third approach of Buddhist Economics through analyzing the influence of Buddhism on economic growth in Asia. His research hypothesizes that Buddhism has "perceptible or unique implications for past and future economic change." He looks into various aspects including Buddhist notions of other-worldliness and the ethics of production and saving, collectivist attributes, transaction costs and economic growth, scientific world-view, tolerance for social and economic change, and so forth. He attempts to analyze Buddhism through its ability to facilitate or constrain economic changes. Still, it is very challenging to account accurately for "Buddhist-influence" and determine how Buddhism affects the socio-economic development of a particular economy in isolation of other values and competing factors. The nature and strength of Buddhist influence are also too wide and diverse to attribute any strong regularity.

He concludes that Buddhism does not necessarily constitute a constraint on economic welfare growth, and the "trade-off" between positive features of the Buddhist world-view is sufficient to "offset" the impediments. In terms of the modern notion of sustainable development, Buddhist values are very consistent. Buddhism's compatibility with economic growth, he argues, could be dependent on the "actual extent and nature of the spillovers associated with the quest for individual material accumulation (Daniels 1998). In economies where negative spillovers of this individual quest are high, Buddhist Economics, which emphasizes "compassion, mindfulness of community impact and minimal environmental impact and consumption," could have a greater chance of maximizing utility regarding sustainable economic growth.

Alexandrin (1993) also offered an elaborated discussion on Buddhist Economics focusing on how ethical elements could be reintegrated into modern economics for social and environmental considerations. He explores in detail the relationship between Buddhism, Socialism, and Marxism as well as its application in some Southeast Asian countries including Thailand, Sri Lanka, Burma, and so forth. Zadek (1993) stated that this third approach to Buddhist Economics may put economic growth as an endogenous variable to be maximized, subject to the "constraint" of Buddhist behaviors. It could be a questionable trade-off between the monastics and the laity and "some enlightenment now, and more enlightenment in the future."

Comparative Study

The fourth approach of Buddhist Economics comprises comparative research by various scholars to tie Buddhist canonical interpretations and meanings to modern economic terms and definitions. Pryor (1990) presented the principles of the Buddhist Economic system by elaborating Buddhist views on property, poverty, and institution in the *Pāli* texts. Payutto (1998) presented his view on how the economy could be operated by discussing the Buddhist Middle Way approach on consumption, production, choice, competition, wealth, and so forth. He contributes further to the behavioral economics discussion by offering a Buddhist perspective on human behaviors and nature in making economic decisions. He presents a direct response to the rational assumption of neoclassical economic theory by understanding the importance of our mental activities leading to the decision.

Similar to the second approach discussed previously, Pryor (1990, 1991) emphasizes that the attainment of *nibbana* is the ultimate objective of Buddhist teachings (understanding the reality of this world, enlightenment bliss), transcending beyond cycles of ignorance and rebirth–the strand related to *nibbana* (Pāli). To achieve this goal of enlightenment, one has to follow the moral teachings of the *Buddha* in everyday mind and bodily actions and accumulate good merits–the kammic strand (Pryor 1990). Both strands are of great relevance to the monastic and lay communities. Accordingly, all economic activities including the benefit of production and consumption should be assessed for their ability to enhance the quality of our life regarding self-development. Concerning the no-self, impermanent and interconnected nature of individuals, society, and our environment, Buddhism advocates contentment and non-attachment to possessions. It calls for a deep ecological thinking to assess our economic behaviors not only for one's immediate self-interest, but also for the interest of society and environment now and in the future. They illustrate the Buddhist Middle Way in achieving a balance between material and spiritual development and avoiding the extreme of self-indulgence and asceticism.

Puntasen (2007a, b, 2008) also makes significant contributions to this comparative approach by analyzing the building blocks of classical economics and Buddhist Economics on topics such as happiness and *paññā*, production, consumption, utility, income distribution, and so forth. He attempts to draw an analogous but alternate path of economic activities driven not by profit, but the elimination of suffering (*dukkha*) and development of happiness (*sukha*). This approach presents a Buddhist Economic model in which *sukha* can be gained through the cultivation of wisdom *Paññā* that requires "no additional resources more than basic necessity" (Puntasen 2007b). He also believes that other Buddhist teachings such as carefulness, non-violence, right livelihood, honesty, and so forth could also be applied to other areas of economic activities (Puntasen 2008).

Like Payutto (1998), Puntasen (2007a, b, 2008), Daniels (2005), Zsolnai (2007, 2011), Alexandrin and Zech (1999) and Alexandrin (1993) compare side-by-side some key features of Buddhist Economics and modern economics to explain how Buddhist Economics could potentially contribute to a new economic model. This perspective of Buddhist Economics, as Daniels (2005) argues, could find its roots in the work of sociologists like Weber in the early twentieth century. It "reverses the causality direction emphasis in the *Homo economius* microeconomic studies of religion and analyzes the economic behavioural and systemic impacts of religion." Weber (1965) focused on "*the relations between* religious ideas and commitments and other aspects of human conduct, especially the economic characteristics of human conduct within a society." Daniels (2005) research is, however, concerned with "how beliefs, norms and values affect economic choices and activities" and their contributions to a deeper understanding of the required changes in economic behaviors which could address current systemic problems in market economy, contributing to true well-being of mankind.

Practical Strategic Models

Daniels (2005) believes that it is possible to develop an alternative system based on principles which are compatible with Buddhist teachings. This focus on developing a practical model to contextualize and integrate Buddhist teachings into the market economy could be categorized as the fifth approach of Buddhist Economics. With a Buddhist philosophical and ethical foundation, he believes that "many widely-appreciated ultimate goals of economic life could be more successfully attained" in an enhanced system. While other scholars adhere to the Buddhist teachings on contentment, other-worldliness and focusing economic activities as a means to meet ultimate spiritual development goals, he focuses on how Buddhist Economics could address some of the problems of the market economy, particularly in relation to his later research on how Buddhist values and the notion of interconnectedness could produce better understanding and changes in environmental protection (Daniels 2003, 2010).

Zadek (1997) contends that Buddhism Economics does not necessarily answer day-to-day economic questions such as inflation, interest rate, and so forth but it does "offer a set of ethical norms that should be followed." Zadek's perspective on Buddhist Economics is a significant guidance in this fifth approach of Buddhist Economics. Buddhist Economics in this sense is engaging, conceptualized in our economy and actionable: "A meaningful Buddhist Economics needs ... to be able to demonstrate a Buddhist Economy" (Zadek 1997).

Along this stream of study, Kovács (2014) presents a Buddhist approach to sustainability by drawing a relationship between the eight United Nations Millennium Development Goals for 2015, and the Threefold Training and the Noble Eightfold Path. He argues that the MDGs' focus on basic necessities is parallel with Buddhist emphasis on food, clothing, shelter, and essential medical care. Although he could, perhaps, elaborate more on the mechanism on which Buddhist teachings could facilitate the achievement of these MDGs, his study contributes to bridging the gap among material economic growth, non-material development goals and the Buddhist teachings.

Tideman's (2004) research in Gross National Happiness ("GNH") was also another attempt to address the non-material qualitative values in economic growth. He explained the Bhutan's leaders' focus on the four pillars of GNH: (1) economic development, (2) good governance, (3) cultural preservation, and (4) nature conservation, but also looks into the complex connection between these qualitative goals and quantifiable policies and measures. He suggests an indirect approach in measuring phenomena relating to happiness and unhappiness because measuring happiness directly "tends to confuse short-term sensory happiness with deeper inner experiences" (2004).

On this fifth approach to Buddhist Economics, a similar model has been introduced in Thailand. Prayukvong (2005) illustrated in a case study of Southern Thailand that successful development of community enterprises could be attributable in part to the Noble Eightfold Path with an emphasis on right understanding and right thought. The Eightfold Path would also fit within the context of a broad-base notion of Sufficiency Economy bestowed by His Majesty the King Bhumibol Adulyadej. This notion of sufficiency means "having enough to live on and to live for" and "building one's strength within proper bounds and reasons" (Punyaboon 2014). It focuses on the well-being, rather than the material wealth, based on a balanced approach to internal and external developments and Buddhist teachings of Middle Way, contentment, and moderate way.

Zsolnai (2009) also contributed to this area of research by presenting the shortfalls of the rational choice model and proposing an alternative qualitative and quantitative Responsible Decision-Making Model. The model allows for the responsibility as an important input. Instead of pure self-interest or utilitarian considerations, Zsolnai established that a decision-maker's set of choices is largely determined by his or her perceived responsibility. In other words, the decision-maker would consider what one "ought to" or "should" do so that one would be responsible, largely in term of moral responsibility, for both the individual and organizations.

There are also other important studies in this aspect of Buddhist Economics. Magnuson (2017) explores the integration of inwardly work on ourselves and outwardly work for true liberation according to

Buddhism. He offers a contemporary discussion on the crises human facing in the economy. Inoue (1997) analyzed some interesting business cases on applying Buddhist philosophy and ethical behaviors, encouraging business leaders to balance inner development with material development. Brown (2017) offers valuable contemporary analyses of Buddhist Economics and the market economy. She emphasizes on the significance of kindness and compassion in changing the way we engage in economic activities.

Chapter Summary

- The *Buddha* is a title to those extraordinary beings awakened to the knowledge of the world through which cessation of suffering is possible. He is not a god but a teacher.
- The historical *Buddha* was born in *Kapilavatthu* more than 2500 years ago. He was the son of a local chieftain.
- He enjoyed a comfortable life but one day he witnessed the impermanence of life and realized that he is also subject to the same impermanence, and mundane pleasures are not solid and worthy.
- He finally gained enlightenment with the insights of the path leading to the cessation of the suffering. Since then he continued to teach his discoveries, the *dhamma*, with a community of disciplined disciples called the *saṅgha*.
- Economics is an evolving subject with many different schools of thought based upon a wide range of assumptions and theories about human behaviors and the world.
- Transactions are the core components contributing to economic activities, where buying and selling occur in exchange for a good, a service, or a financial asset.
- Humans have different motivations behinds transactions. Human nature affects economic conditions, and vice versa.
- Buddhist Economics as a field of research has at least five approaches, namely (1) canonical review, (2) alternative visions and paths, (3) analyses on the economic arrangements of Buddhist related institutions, (4) comparative study; and (5) practical strategic models.
- To demonstrate the relevance of Buddhist values in contemporary economy and society, this book focuses on the fourth and fifth approaches.

Study Questions

- Is it possible for a human being to become a *Buddha*?
- How is the economic model presented by Dalio different from your daily experience?
- What are the key different approaches on the subject on Buddhist Economics?
- In each different approach, how the study of Buddhism interacts with economic theories to form an interdisciplinary subject?

Suggested Essay Topics

- *Buddha* as a teacher and a healer
- A brief account of the life of the *Buddha*
- The triple gems of Buddhism: the *Buddha*, *dhamma*, and *saṅgha*
- How the economic machine works?
- Core components of the market economy

Bibliography

Online Multimedia

BDEP. 2015. Life of Buddha. In Buddha's Birthday Education Project. https://www.youtube.com/watch?v=Q9R-cqf6Pmk

Dalio, Ray. 2013. How the Economic Machine Works. https://www.youtube.com/watch?v=PheObXAIuk0

Required Reading

Cantwell, Cathy. 2010. The Buddha and the Roots of the Buddhist Tradition. In *Buddhism: The Basics*, 19–55. London/New York: Routledge.

Dalio, Ray. 2015. How the Economic Machine Works. http://www.economicprinciples.org/wp-content/uploads/ray_dalio__how_the_economic_machine_works__leveragings_and_deleveragings.pdf. Accessed 1 Dec 2015.

Gethin, Rupert. 1998. The Buddha: The Story of the Awakened One. In *The Foundations of Buddhism*, 7–34. Oxford/New York: Oxford University Press.

Further Reading

Abeynayake, Oliver. 2016. *The Social and Economic Dimensions of Early Buddhism*. Hong Kong: The Buddha-Dharma Centre of Hong Kong.

Alexandrin, Glen. 1993. Elements of Buddhist Economics. *International Journal of Social Economics* 20 (2): 3–11.

Alexandrin, Glen, and Charles E. Zech. 1999. Ancient Futures: Papal and Buddhist Economics. *International Journal of Social Economics* 26 (10/11): 1344–1353.
Brown, Clair. 2017. *Buddhist Economics*. New York: Bloomsbury Press.
Cantwell, Cathy. 2010. The Buddha's Life Story. In *Buddhism: The Basics*, 24–41, 54 London/New York: Routledge.
Chang, Ha-Joon. 2014. *Economics: The User's Guide*. London: Pelican, Penguin Books.
Chang, Otto H. 2006. The Buddhist Approach to Economic Development: The Path to A Wisdom-based Economy. *Hsi Lai Journal of Humanistic Buddhism* 7: 173–181.
Daniels, Peter L. 1998. Economic Change, the Environment and Buddhism in Asia. *International Journal of Social Economics* 25 (6/7/8): 968–1004.
———. 2003. Buddhist Economics and the Environment: Material Flow Analysis and the Moderation of Society's Metabolism. *International Journal of Social Economics* 30 (1/2): 8–33.
———. 2005. Economic Systems and the Buddhist World View: The 21st Century Nexus. *The Journal of Socio-Economics* 34: 245–268.
———. 2010. Climate Change, Economics and Buddhism—Part 2: New Views and Practices for Sustainable World Economies. *Ecological Economics* 69 (5): 962–972.
Essen, Juliana. 2010. Sufficiency Economy and Santi Asoke: Buddhist Economic Ethics for a Just and Sustainable World. *Journal of Buddhist Ethics* 17: 69–99.
Gethin, Rupert. 1998. The Buddha: The Story of the Awakened One. In *The Foundations of Buddhism*, 7–27. Oxford/New York: Oxford University Press.
Harvey, Peter. 2000. Economic Ethics. In *An Introduction to Buddhist Ethics: Foundations, Values and Issues*, 187–237. Cambridge: Cambridge University Press. Reprint, Seventh.
———. 2013. The Buddha and His Indian Context. In *An Introduction to Buddhism: Teachings, History and Practices*, 2nd ed., 8–29. New York: Cambridge University Press. Original edition, 1990.
Hettiarachchi, Dharmasena. 2001. *Buddhist Economic Philosophy: As Reflected in Early Buddhism*. Trans. Sanath Nanayakkara. Colombo: Educational Publications Department.
Hwang, Kwang-Kuo. 2015. Dual Belief in Heaven and Spirits: The Metaphysical Foundation of Confucian Morality. In *Routledge Handbook of Religions in Asia*, ed. Bryan S. Turner and Oscar Salemink. Oxon/New York: Routledge.
Inoue, Shinichi. 1997. *Putting Buddhism to Work: A New Approach to Management and Business*. Trans. Duncan R. Williams. Tokyo: Kodansha International Ltd. Original edition, in Japanese, Chikyu o Suku'u Keizaigaku 1994 by Suzuku Shuppan, Tokyo.
Kovács, Gábor. 2014. Buddhist Approach to Sustainability and Achieving Millennium Development Goals. In *The 11th of International Buddhist Conference on the United Nations Day of Vesak (2014/2557), Cat Bai Dinh Temple*. Ninh Binh: Vietnam.

Magnuson, Joel. 2011. *Mindful Economics: How the US Economy Works, Why It Matters, and How It Could Be Different.* New York: Seven Stories Press.

———. 2017. *From Greed to Wellbeing: A Buddhist Approach to Resolving Our Economic and Financial Crises.* Bristol: Policy Press.

MLDB. MN 26. Ariyapariyesanā: The Noble Search. In *MLDB*, 253–268. Somerville: Wisdom Publications.

MLDB. MN 36. Mahāsaccaka Sutta: The Greater Discourse to Saccaka. In *MLDB*, 332–343. Somerville: Wisdom Publications.

MLDB. MN 7. Vatthūpama Sutta: The Simile of the Cloth. In *MLDB*, 118–122. Wisdom Publications: Somerville.

Ñanamoli, Bhikkhu, and Bhikkhu Bodhi. 1995. *The Middle Length Discourses of the Buddha: A Translation of the Majjhima Nikaya (Teachings of the Buddha).* Somerville: Wisdom Publications.

Nanayakkara, S. K. 1995. Social Dimensions of Buddhism. In *Encyclopedia of Buddhism.* Extract No. 3, ed. W. G. Weeraratne. Padukka: The State Printing Corporation.

Ng, Ernest C.H. 2015. *Buddhist Perspectives on Economic Growth: A Buddhist-based Sustainable Investment Model Within Market Economy.* Thesis, University of Hong Kong.

Payutto, PA. 1998. *Buddhist Economics, A Middle Way for the Market Place.* Bangkok: Buddhadhamma Foundation.

Prayukvong, Wanna. 2005. A Buddhist Economic Approach to the Development of Community Enterprises: A Case Study from Southern Thailand. *Cambridge Journal of Economics* 29 (6): 1171–1185.

Pryor, Frederic L. 1990. A Buddhist Economic system—in Principle. *American Journal of Economics and Sociology* 49 (3): 339–349.

———. 1991. A Buddhist Economic System. In Practice: The Rules of State Policy Making of the Ideal King's Sought a "Middle Way" Between Right and Left. *American Journal of Economics and Sociology* 50 (1): 17–32.

Puntasen, Apichai. 2007a. Buddhist Economics as a New Paradigm Towards Happiness. *Society and Economy* 29 (2): 181–200.

———. 2007b. *Why Buddhist Economics Is Needed as a New Paradigm for a Better Understanding of Happiness (Wellness).* International Conference on Happiness and Public Policy, Bangkok.

———. 2008. *Buddhist Economics: Evolution, Theories, and Its Application to Various Economics Subjects.* Bangkok: Amarin Publisher.

Punyaboon, Rachroat. 2014. Sufficiency Economy: An Innovative Method of Buddhist Development Economics. *Journal of Humanities and Social Sciences* 3 (2): 33–54.

Rahula, Basnagoda Bhikkhu. 2008. *The Buddha's Teachings on Prosperity: At Home, at Work, in the World.* Boston: Wisdom Publications.

Reynolds, Frank E., and Regina T. Clifford. 1980. Sangha, Society, and the Struggle for National Identity: Burma and Thailand. In *Transitions and Transformations in the History of Religions: Essays in honor of Joseph M. Kitagawa*, ed. Frank E. Reynolds and Theodore M. Ludwig, 56–91. Leiden: E. J. Brill.

Schumacher, Ernst F. 1984. *Small Is Beautiful: Economics as if People Mattered*. London: Sphere Books Ltd. Original edition, 1973.

Sivaraksa, Sulak. 2011. *The Wisdom of Sustainability: Buddhist Economics for the 21st Century*. Asheville: Koa Books.

Tideman, Sander G. 2004. *Gross National Happiness: Towards a New Paradigm in Economics*. First International Conference on Operationalization of Gross National Happiness, Bhutan.

Weber, Max. 1965. *The Sociology of Religion*. Trans. Ephraim Fischoff. First English translation from the Fourth Edition ed. London: Methuen & Co Ltd. Original edition, 1922 by J.C.B. Mohr in Germany.

———. 1978. *Economy and Society: An Outline of Interpretive Sociology*. California: University of California Press.

Zadek, Simon. 1993. The Practice of Buddhist Economics? Another View. *American Journal of Economics and Sociology* 52 (4): 433–445.

———. 1997. Towards a Progressive Buddhist Economics. In *Entering the Realm of Reality: Towards Dharmmic Societies*, ed. Jonathan Watts, Alan Senauke, and Santikaro Bhikkhu, 241–277. Bangkok: INEB.

Zsolnai, László. 2007. Western Economics Versus Buddhist Economics. *Society and Economy* 29 (2): 145–153.

———. 2009. *Responsible Decision Making*. In *Praxiology: The International Annual of Practical Philosophy and Methodology*, ed. Wojciech W. Gasparski. Transaction Publishers: New Brunswick.

———. 2011. Buddhist Economics. In *Handbook of Spirituality and Business*, 88–94. London: Palgrave Macmillan.

CHAPTER 2

The Four Noble Truths: A Decision-Making and Problem-Solving Framework

The Four Noble Truths

Early *sutta* presented the *Buddha*'s teachings as the solution to one of the most important problem in human life, being the cessation of suffering. The *Buddha*'s first teaching at *Bārāṇasi*, as recorded in the Setting in Motion the Wheel of the Dhamma (Pāli: *Dhammacakkappavattana Sutta*) (CDB. SN 56.11), addressed this through the Four Noble Truths: (1) the truth of suffering, (2) the truth of the origination of suffering, (3) the truth of the cessation of suffering, and (4) the truth of the path to the cessation of suffering. The Four Noble Truths occupy a central role in Buddhist teachings.

"Noble" refers to those who are noble, like the *Buddha* or others on the path to enlightenment, and the path itself. "Truths" are essentially the truth as seen by these Noble Ones. People, however, often misunderstand the Truths to be absolute claims one must believe in order to become a Buddhist. This misconstruction is encouraged by the word "truth." The *Pāli* term *sacca* can be translated to mean truth, but it can also be defined as "real" or "actual thing." The Four Truths are not statement that we must either agree or disagree with, but rather four "true things" or "realities" whose nature the *Buddha* understood upon enlightenment. Hence, the Truths are more a rough conceptual framework for understanding Buddhist teachings instead of a strict doctrine. The Truths simply open one's eyes to the knowledge "as it is" or "as it should be."

E. C. H. Ng, *Introduction to Buddhist Economics*,
Studies in Buddhist Economics, Management, and Policy,
https://doi.org/10.1007/978-3-030-35114-4_2

The *Buddha* taught us to confirm or evaluate his teachings through our experience. It is this confirmation process that one must develop "a sound basis for placing faith" in other aspects of his teachings, which may initially transcend beyond our ordinary experience. It is from wisdom in ordinary experience that we develop the leap of faith which allows us to gain confidence in his teachings, which are supposed to take us to a higher level of wisdom to continue this journey of transformation.

Buddha's own quest for the enlightenment began when he realized, even with everything he could ever want and possess, he and his loved ones were subject to disease, old age, and death; and so true happiness was out of reach. The *Buddha* is frequently described as a doctor and the Four Noble Truths as the medical diagnosis. The truth of suffering is the disease, the origin of suffering is the cause, the truth of cessation is the suffering being cured, and the path to cessation is the medicine that brings about the cure. The Fourth Noble Truth is the "path" (Pāli: *magga*) or "way" (Pāli: *paṭipadā*). Buddhism is not so much a religion in the strictest definition of the term but more as a "system of training in conduct, meditation, and wisdom" (Gethin 1998) that leads to the cessation of suffering as the paramount objective. As this chapter illustrates, the Four Noble Truths could be understood through a problem-solving and decision-making framework, with the "suffering" behind the problem, the "cause" being the origin behind the problem, the "cessation" being the solution to the problem, whereas the "Path" is the practical guide to solve the solution.

The Four Noble Truths taught by the *Buddha* are as much about the cessation of suffering as they are about happiness, which are like two sides of the same coin. Buddhist analysis of suffering is not pessimistic but optimistic; by understanding suffering clearly, we will no longer confuse it with happiness or vice versa. We gain faith in the fact that there are different levels of happiness, accessible to all through practicing the Noble Eightfold Path and guided by moral discipline, concentration, and wisdom. It is only when we realize the true nature of happiness, the origin of happiness, and the path leading to happiness that we can truly alleviate suffering. If the *Buddha* offers great inspiration for those going through the unavoidable ups and downs of life, his teachings should also offer some great insights for decision-making in the market economy, offer solution and practical model for the cessation of suffering in the market economy (Fig. 2.1).

Fig. 2.1 Sand Mandala (*Tangkas Mandala*). Note: Monastics creating a sand mandala which depicts Buddhist teachings and world-view. (Source: Photo by author)

Suffering: The Problem

As Bodhi (2013) argues the problem of suffering is "the very cornerstone of [the *Buddha*'s] teaching." Suffering (Pāli: *dukkha*) taught by the *Buddha*, however, is not simply pain and misery. It refers to the fundamental "unsatisfactoriness running through our lives." All living beings experience suffering. Within Buddhist philosophy analysis, it applies to the entirety of conditioned existence.

Suffering can be broken down into three different levels: (1) the suffering of suffering, which refers to physical pain (such as birth, aging, death, sickness, accidents, injuries, hunger and thirst) or mental reactions to disagreeable situations and events in sorrow, anger, frustration, fear aroused by painful separations, by unpleasant encounters, by the failure to get what we want (Bodhi 2013); (2) the suffering of change, referring to the loss of a desirable condition or the appearance of an undesirable condition, for everything is ultimately impermanent (Pāli: *anicca*). If we expect pleasant conditions last forever, we are destined to be disappointed; (3) the pervasive suffering of conditioned existence or suffering of the impermanence of life. The suffering that "seems to be inherent in the nature of our existence—*dukkha* as conditions" (Gethin 1998).

Cause: Origin of the Problem

People may recognize suffering, even if they cannot identify the cause. Some view Buddhism as a rather pessimistic philosophy due to its emphasis on suffering, but a Buddhist perspective would view such claims as a deep-rooted refusal to accept the reality of suffering and signifies a misunderstanding of the *Buddha*'s teachings. It is the ignorance of suffering and its causes.

The root of suffering is craving. It can be craving for "satisfaction, happiness, success, material acquisition, and for the avoidance of unpleasant conditions, poverty, loss, blame, and so forth" (Cantwell 2010). The inability to attain one's craving can lead to suffering. Alternatively, the obtainment of happiness at the expense of the happiness of others can lead to bad *kamma* and also result in long-term suffering.

The act of craving and attachment is far more important than the object of craving and attachment itself. For instance, Buddhist followers do not harm living creatures not because of some attachment to an ethical principle, but because they have rid themselves of any motivation that would lead them to do so.

An occasional addition to the Second Truth includes craving driven by ignorance (Pāli: *avijjā*) which hinders our clear perception. The chain of craving can be broken either at the first link, ignorance, or the eighth link, craving. Even without craving, we fail to see things as they really are due to a muddled and confused mind. We get upset when events or the external world operate different from our expectation. We mistakenly assume that we will be happy if our craving is satisfied, but this judgment additionally presupposes a world in where everything is permanent, stable, and reliable.

Buddhist philosophy suggests that the three fundamental defilements of the mind are: greed (Pāli: *rāga, lobha*), aversion (Pāli: *dosa*), and ignorance (Pāli: *avijjā, moha*) (Gethin 1998). They interact and manifest in different ways to produce suffering. Only by letting go of all craving can suffering be eliminated.

Cessation: Solution to the Problem

Suffering can be ceased through the removal of craving. Conditioned existence is whatever unconditioned existence is not. It is impossible to describe the state of unconditioned existence; one must experience it for themselves. Buddhist thought also proposes individuals must take ultimate responsibility for their suffering. While seemingly gloomy, it relates to the Third and Fourth Truths. In an ever-changing world, the thirst for repeated existence is futile. Suffering is caused by our own craving and hence, we are able to resolve it.

The ultimate goal of the Buddhist path is *nibbana* (Pāli): true happiness with the cessation of suffering. It is not a "thing" but an event or experience. Upon attainment, the mind is purged of the three fundamental defilements and enters the unconditioned realm known at the moment of awakening. It is also the final condition of the *Buddha* and *arahant*-s after death. Nirvana is neither existence nor non-existence. To firmly lock it into either one state goes against the Buddhist idea of steering a middle course transcending above "the annihilationist view (Pāli: *uccheda-vāda*) and the eternalist view (Pāli: *sassatavāda*)" (Gethin 1998).

Karunadasa (2015a) emphasizes the end of suffering (Pāli: *nibbana*) is not the end of the world, but the cessation of a wrong interpretation and construction of the world "through the lens of our ego-centric perspectives: our views and beliefs, our speculative theories and dogmatic assertions" leading to suffering. Hence, the *Buddha* explained that theoretical views (Pāli: *diṭṭhi*) using the framework of the Four Noble Truths: (1) views, (2) origin of views (Pāli: *diṭṭhi-samudaya*), (3) cessation of views (Pāli: *diṭṭhi-nirodha*), and (4) the path that leads to the cessation of views (Pāli: *diṭṭhi-nirodha-gāmini paṭipadā*). The "freedom from views" (Pāli: *diṭṭhi-nissaraṇa*) is, in fact, another expression for *nibbana* (Pāli), suggesting that the "cessation of views" is the "cessation of suffering" (Karunadasa 2015a).

Cessation of views does not mean not "to view," but to view "as it is" by not having a view (Karunadasa 2015b). To better understand the causes and consequences of our decisions, and how we individually and collectively with millions of other decision-makers are affected emotionally, physically, and financially, we need to view economic phenomena accurately and clearly as they are. We need to view without having "a view," by embracing the Buddhist understanding of impermanence, suffering, and selflessness. Accordingly, we can understand how our ego and the inflated-self drive decisions and activities in the market economy.

Path: Practical Guide to Solve the Problem

The path to the cessation of suffering is the Fourth Noble Truth. It comprises eight "right" aspects including view, intention (resolve/thought), speech, action, livelihood, effort, mindfulness, and concentration (meditative absorption). Each of them is described as "right"—not in the typical sense of "right", as being "good" or "correct" but in the sense that it is whole, complete or perfect (Pāli: *sammā*).

Bodhi (2013) expounds that each of the Four Noble Truths and the Noble Eightfold Path, being the essence of the teaching of the *Buddha*, covers the doctrinal side and disciplinary side, respectively. While the Four Noble Truths inspire intellectual understanding, the Noble Eightfold Path guides practice. They are intertwined with the Fourth Noble Truths being the Noble Eightfold Path; and the first Noble Eightfold Path, the right view, being the proper understanding of the Four Noble Truths. Without a proper approach and understanding, the eight aspects of the Noble Eightfold Path cannot be perfected. The Four Noble Truths and the Noble Eightfold Path work in harmony, deepening understanding with practice (Bodhi 2013). In another formulation, the Threefold Training of moral discipline, mental concentration, and wisdom could also be linked to the Noble Eightfold Path. However, the Threefold Training is slightly more inclusive and has an institutionalized schema that is suitable for all, while the Eightfold Path was initially conceptualized for committed renouncers as seen by its presentation in the *Dhammacakkappavattana Sutta*.

To achieve moral discipline on the Noble Eightfold Path, right speech, right action and right livelihood are the necessary practices to train our mind and bodily actions, our speech and our means of living. Mental concentration is achieved in the Noble Eightfold Path through right effort, right concentration, and right mindfulness. In other words, it means that mental concentration requires the right effort (methodology and striving) to apply the right focus on the right objects (of meditation). Wisdom is achieved in the Noble Eightfold Path through right view and right intention. Right view is the understanding of the cause and effect of a relationship as discussed above. Once we have established the right understanding, it is important to maintain right intention undisturbed by obstacles or distractions.

Bodhi (2013) analyzed that the right view and right intention is at the beginning of the Noble Eightfold Path, while wisdom comprising right view and right intention at the end of the Threefold Training is not contradictory at all. In the Noble Eightfold Path, right view and right intention set up the proper perspective and direction for the practice at the beginning, while the right view and right intention in the Threefold Training are the higher superior level wisdom supported by the trainings of moral discipline and mental concentration. In the *Discourse on Right View Sutta* (*Sammaditthi Sutta*), *Sariputta* elaborates that right view is considered in relation to wholesomeness, nutriment, the Four Noble Truths, and the Doctrine of Dependent Origination (MLDB. MN 9). In other words, right view is assessed with respect to how we perceive the nature of reality and morality.

As Prayukvong (2005) suggests, right intention is to direct thoughts in "positive and helpful directions," objectively without desire or bias and hence, constructive actions could be taken. It will reinforce a series of other positive steps along the path. The *Buddha* explains that right intention includes that of renunciation, good will, and harmlessness, they correspond to the wrong intention of desire, ill will, and harmfulness (Bodhi 2013).

The path factors of right speech, right action, and right livelihood correspond to the moral discipline of the Threefold Training. In fact, moral disciplines in Buddhist Philosophy are not far-fetched, unrealistic ideals but concrete living principles applicable to everyone concerning the way we act, communicate, and think. The principles behind the right speech, right action, and right livelihood are established on the practical wisdom that we should behave so that we can protect our own well-being and that of others. The rights and wrongs, or the dos and don'ts, do not mean simply obeying orders from higher authorities, customs, popular views, or the rule of law; they are fundamental guidelines that can contribute to our well-being. In the *Kālāma Sutta*, the *Buddha* taught us not to subject ourselves to authority and popular views, but to assess what is morally wholesome to ourselves (NDB. AN 3.65):

> Come, Kālāmas, do not go by oral tradition … But when you know for yourselves: 'These things are wholesome; these things are blameless; these things are praised by the wise; these things, if accepted and undertaken, lead to welfare and happiness,' then you should live in accordance with them.

Our well-being is ultimately governed by the quality of our mind: our behaviors are skillful if they are consistent with the practice of generosity, compassion, wisdom; they are not skillful if our mind is defiled by greed, hatred, and ignorance. The Threefold Training corresponds to the training for our body and mind: in the way we behave through right speech, right action, and right livelihood in the Noble Eightfold Path; in the way we perceive and conceive through right effort, right concentration, and right mindfulness; and ultimately in the way our consciousness operates through right view and right intention.

Even though our verbal and bodily actions are manifestations of our mental activities, our minds and thoughts are difficult to detect or monitor. Once our thoughts are expressed outwardly into speech or writing, they can be observed. While both can cause damage, harmful speech is comparatively less destructive than bodily action because physical damage is somewhat irreversible, and the associated sensory experience can leave a long-lasting imprint on our mind. Often our experiences can drive an upward spiral propelling further actions and reactions back to our conceptions and perceptions. Since physical actions are easier to monitor and control than mental activity, they are considered the frontier of moral discipline. We must realize that our mind cannot be truly free if our actions, perceptions, and mental activities are not under our control but are enslaved and entangled by our greed, hatred, and ignorance.

The training of mental concentration is achieved through right effort, right mindfulness, and right concentration of the Noble Eightfold Path. It is through mental concentration which wisdom could be cultivated because the mind has to be calm and focused. Right concentration allows the mind to be stable, unified, and pay undivided attention to the suitable and stable object of awareness. It is only be possible with the support of right effort which is the vigor or energy required to support right concentration on the right mindfulness. Unlike normal state of consciousness, our mind residing in the right mindfulness achieves a tranquil and open state of "bare attention, a detached observation of what is happening within us and around us in the present moment" (Bodhi 2013).

To fully develop wisdom that could lead us to the cessation of suffering, the Noble Eightfold Path does not end with the right mindfulness (Table 2.1). It is through the practice of all eight factors in the Noble Eightfold Path which the right view and the right intention are taken to a higher level of realization and deepening, ultimately leading to the deep insight into the nature of human defilements and sufferings, seeing our "self" and the external world "as it is."

Table 2.1 The Noble Eightfold Path

Threefold training	*Noble eightfold path*	*Practices*
Wisdom	Right view (right understanding)	Understanding suffering Understanding its origin Understanding its cessation Understanding the way leading to its cessation
	Right intention (resolve/ thought)	Intention of renunciation Intention of good will Intention of harmlessness
Moral discipline	Right speech	Abstaining from false speech Abstaining from slanderous speech Abstaining from harsh speech Abstaining from idle chatter
	Right action	Abstaining from taking life Abstaining from stealing Abstaining from sexual misconduct
	Right livelihood	Giving up wrong livelihood (that contradict right speech and right action) One earns one's living by a right form of livelihood
Mental concentration	Right effort	Effort to retrain defilements Effort to abandon defilements Effort to develop wholesome states Effort to maintain wholesome
	Right mindfulness	Mindful contemplation of the body Mindful contemplation of the feelings Mindful contemplation of the mind Mindful contemplation of the dhammas (phenomena)
	Right concentration (meditative absorption)	The first meditation state (*jhāna*) The second meditation state The third meditation state The fourth meditation state

Source: Author with reference to Bodhi (2013) and Gethin (1998)

Chapter Summary

- The Four Noble Truths are parts of the most important teachings of the *Buddha* which addresses the core question of human life, being the cessation of suffering.
- The Four Noble Truths are: (1) the truth of suffering, (2) the truth of the origination of suffering, (3) the truth of the cessation of suffering, and (4) the truth of the path to the cessation of suffering.

- "Noble" refers to those who are noble, like the *Buddha* or others on the path to enlightenment, and the path itself. "Truths" are essentially the truth "as it is" seen by these Noble Ones.
- Suffering (Pāli: *dukkha*) refers to the fundamental "unsatisfactoriness" in lives of all sentient beings. It could be understood from the level of (1) suffering of suffering, (2) suffering of change, and (3) suffering of conditioned existence.
- Cause of suffering is craving and ignorance. The three fundamental defilements of the mind are greed (Pāli: *rāga, lobha*), aversion (Pāli: *dosa*), and ignorance (Pāli: *avijjā, moha*).
- Suffering can be ceased through the removal of craving. The goal of the Buddhist path is *nibbana* (Pāli): true happiness with the cessation of suffering.
- The path to the cessation of suffering comprises eight "right" aspects including view, intention (resolve/thought), speech, action, livelihood, effort, mindfulness, and concentration (meditative absorption). They are "right" not in the typical sense as being "good" or "correct" but in the sense that it is whole, complete or perfect (Pāli: *sammā*).
- The Threefold Training of moral discipline, mental concentration, and wisdom are also manifested in the Noble Eightfold Path which contribute to the cultivation of wisdom and ultimately the cessation of suffering.

Study Questions

- How is the Buddhist notion of truth different from the conventional truth?
- Explain the sequence of the Four Noble Truths and Noble Eightfold Path.
- Why does the *Buddha* consider his realization of the Four Noble Truths difficult for humans to appreciate?
- Why is the right view "right"?

Suggested Essay Topics

- The Four Noble Truths as a decision-making and problem-solving framework
- Notion of suffering and its origin

- Cessation of suffering through the Noble Eightfold Path
- The relationship between the Four Noble Truths and the Noble Eightfold Path

Bibliography

Required Reading

Bhikkhu Bodhi. 2013. The Noble Eightfold Path: The Way to the End of Suffering. Access to Insight (BCBS Edition). Last modified 30 Nov 2013. http://www.accesstoinsight.org/lib/authors/bodhi/waytoend.html

Cantwell, Cathy. 2010. The Four Truths of the Noble Ones. In *Buddhism: The Basics*, 61–68. London/New York: Routledge.

Gethin, Rupert. 1998. Four Truths: The Disease, the Cause, the Cure, the Medicine. In *The Foundations of Buddhism*, 59–79. Oxford/New York: Oxford University Press.

Further Reading

Bodhi, Bhikkhu. 2000. *The Connected Discourses of the Buddha, a Translation of the Saṃyutta Nikāya*. Somerville: Wisdom Publications.

———. 2012. *The Numerical Discourses of the Buddha: A Translation of the Aṅguttara Nikāya*. Translated by from the Pali by Bhikkhu Bodhi. Somerville: Wisdom Publications.

CDB. SN 56.11. *Saccasaṃyutta* (Connected Discourses on the Truths), *Dhammacakkappavattana Sutta* (Setting in Motion the Wheel of the Dhamma). In *CDB*, 1843–1847. Somerville: Wisdom Publications.

Karunadasa, Yakupitiyage. 2015a. *Early Buddhist Teachings: The Middle Position in Theory and Practice*. Hong Kong: Centre of Buddhist Studies, The University of Hong Kong.

———. 2015b. The Role of Meditation in the Threefold Scheme of Buddhist Mental Culture. In *Buddhist Meditative Praxis: Traditional Teachings & Modern Applications*, ed. K.L. Dhammajoti, 117–122. Hong Kong: Centre of Buddhist Studies, The University of Hong Kong.

MLDB. MN 9. Sammādiṭṭhi Sutta: Right View. In *MLDB*, 132–149. Somerville: Wisdom Publications.

Ñanamoli, Bhikkhu, and Bhikkhu Bodhi. 1995. *The Middle Length Discourses of the Buddha: A Translation of the Majjhima Nikaya (Teachings of the Buddha)*. Somerville: Wisdom Publications.

NDB. AN 3.65. Kesaputtiya. In *NDB*, 279–283. Somerville: Wisdom Publications.

Prayukvong, Wanna. 2005. A Buddhist Economic Approach to the Development of Community Enterprises: A Case Study from Southern Thailand. *Cambridge Journal of Economics* 29 (6): 1171–1185.

PART II

The Suffering

CHAPTER 3

What Is the Problem with the Market Economy?

Economics as a Subject: An Evolving Subject with Many Schools of Thought

Economics is a complex subject which definition has evolved over time. Different definitions have influenced the focus and methodology of different fields of economic studies—as fields change, so do the definitions (Backhouse and Medema 2008). The original term *oikonomikos* in Greek means "household management" (Tideman 2004), which was later extended beyond the household to cover the whole nation under the subject of "political economy" in the eighteenth century (Backhouse and Medema 2008). For example, Steuart (1767) suggested that political economy is "first to adapt the different operations of [the state] to the spirit, manners, habits and customs of the people, and afterwards to model these circumstances so, as to be able to introduce a set of new and more useful institutions". On the other hand, Smith (1843) positioned it "as a branch of the science of a statesman or legislator, proposes two distinct objects; first, to provide a plentiful revenue or subsistence for the people, or, more properly, to enable them to provide such a revenue or subsistence for themselves; and, secondly, to supply the state or commonwealth with a revenue sufficient for the public services. It proposes to enrich both the people and the sovereign."

E. C. H. Ng, *Introduction to Buddhist Economics*,
Studies in Buddhist Economics, Management, and Policy,
https://doi.org/10.1007/978-3-030-35114-4_3

Economics was defined by earlier scholars primarily in relation to wealth—"the real value of the annual produce of the land and labor of mankind" (Smith 1843). Jean Baptiste considered the subject as a "treatise on political economy, or a simple account of the way in which wealth is formed, distributed and consumed" (Backhouse and Medema 2008). Mill (1967) described it as the "science which treats of the production and distribution of wealth, so far as they depend upon the laws of human nature" or the "science relating to the moral or psychological laws of the production and distribution of wealth". While these definitions emphasize wealth, Marshall (1890) defined the subject based on well-being:

> Political Economy or Economics is a study of mankind in the ordinary business of life; it examines that part of individual and social action which is most closely connected with the attainment and with the use of the material requisites of wellbeing.

In a simplified model, economic activities in capitalism could have a general objective of achieving economic growth through various forms of decision-making. These decisions involve how we deploy our time and labor in exchange for salary, invest our pay into financial instruments in exchange for capital gain, save today for a return tomorrow, and so forth. Marshall and many scholars of his generation considered it important to study human behaviors, particularly how economic activities influenced characters and hence behaviors (Backhouse and Medema 2008). Robbins took a similar stance on behaviors. He defined economics as "the science which studies human behavior as a relationship between ends and scarce means which have alternative uses" (Robbins 1935). This focus on behaviors and choices, in turn, leads economics to increasingly pay attention to the methodology or the science behind that choice. As Samuelson (1967) defined economics as "the study of how man and society choose, with or without the use of money, to employ scarce product resources, which could have alternative uses, to produce various commodities over time and distribute them for consumption, now and in the future, among various people and groups in society."

The factors driving economic activities are complicated as they involve not only the ends but also the means. Chang (2014) explains that there are at least nine different schools of thought. These schools of thought have different views on the composition of the economy, the individuals, how certain the world is, how policy should be made, how economies should be developed, and so forth. These nine schools are: Classical, Neoclassical, Marxist, Developmentalist, Austrian, Schumpeterian, Keynesian, Institutionalist and the Behaviorist respectively.

These different schools of thought also have different assumptions on who individuals are. For example, the Classical and Neoclassical schools believe that individuals are selfish and rational. The Neoclassical theory, in particular, assumes individuals to be *homo economicus*: selfish and rational beings, believing in the certainties of this world and calculable risks. An individual's focus on maximizing self-interest in the form of utility is the driving force of the economy, which is in turn reliant upon the dominant role of the market exchange and consumption (Chang 2014).

Since some of the Neoclassical economic assumptions listed above fail to explain observed economic behaviors fully, the Behaviorist economic models attempted to better explain the basis and motives of human economic decision and behaviors. The Behaviorist school believes that individuals only have bounded rationality and are layered entities, made up of instinct, habit, belief and reason (Chang 2014). Indeed, further studies on irrational human behaviors in economic activities were conducted and supported the Behaviorist' arguments. Levitt and List (2008) demand the development of a unified theory integrating different behavioral models and empirical results. Behaviorist economic models and studies have to be more "empirically relevant." The research results should be tested in naturally occurring settings as opposed to the laboratory.

In practice, there is no definitive boundary between these schools of economic thought. Chang (2014) believes that one "can justify any government policy, any corporate strategy, or any individual action with the help of Neoclassical economics." These nine schools can be developed into new schools of thought to better explain or predict the economy. He posits that "economics is a political argument." It is not a science in the sense that there is no single truth.

Box 3.1 Ten Core Principles of Economics

Mankiw (2012) offers ten core principles of economics from three perspectives of the individual decision-making, interactions among people, and the economy as a whole. For individual decision-making, the first principle is that people need to make choices among different alternatives leading to different goals. Second, there are trade-offs among these choices and the cost can be considered to be the forgone opportunities. Third, economics assumes that rational people make decisions by comparing marginal costs and marginal benefits. Fourth, people change their behaviors in response to incentives. In terms of the interaction among individuals, the fifth principle suggests that overall trade can benefit everyone involve. In normal circumstance, the sixth principle suggests that markets are preferable common place for transactions. Governments could sometimes make market more efficient is the seventh principal. Interact and transact with each other through trade in a common place known as the market. Trade increases the level of interdependence, but can also be mutually beneficial. It is through the market that economic activities can be coordinated and structured. They can also be facilitated by the government through various institutions and required infrastructure. Overall, living standards of society can be improved through productivity (and employment) is the eighth principle. The ninth principle suggests that the notional value of money earned can be affected by the quantity of money circulated and hence the level of inflation. Society faces a short-term trade-off between the notional value of money (inflation) and unemployment is the tenth one.

The Religion of the Market Economy: When Spirituality and Materiality Intersect

To understand human economic behaviors and interactions, economic studies have sought insights from social science, psychology and even religion. Indeed, religion has made pivotal contributions to the history of economic growth. The interaction between economic pursuit as a new religion and traditional religions is intriguing. Given their teachings on contentment, spiritual developments, and generosity, traditional religion appears to be contradictory to the maximization, material developments and self-centered motivations of the market economy.

There are many different ways to define a religion. A functionalist view suggests that religion serves as a tool to understand "what the world is, and what our role in the world is" (Loy 1997). The market economy could be considered as a new religion of modern times, which attempts to provide an explanation of the world through science and expresses its core values through consumerism (Loy 1997). People are always in search of a Big Other—a God or authority to address their "anxiety of choice," to an extent even willing to give up their conscious decision making to the new governing rules of rational economic theory and consumerism (Salecl 2010). Accordingly, the market is the god of the economy and salvation is achieved through growth with more and more production and consumption—"buy me if you want to be happy" (Loy 1997).

Submitting to the authority of the market "God" seems to require us to take economic relationships as something natural and inevitable: it is right and just and value can be adequately defined by prices in the market. The market should be entrusted to operate without any government intervention, according to the laissez-faire principle, except for certain laws and policies required to allow the market to function properly. Nonetheless, Loy (1997) reminded us that the market relationships we now take for granted are in fact dependent on many socio-cultural factors. For example, certain character traits such as trust are required for the market to work properly. Not only does the market rely on the community to generate the moral capital required to support the market, it seems to exploit the moral capital available in society as well, just as the market takes the environment for granted. The erosion of "moral capital" is a term economist use to describe the moral trade-off which people seem to be willing to engage in for more monetary and financial capital.

Having reviewed the success of developed markets versus the rest of the world, Ferguson (2011) concluded that their successes could be attributed to six "killer apps." These six "identifiably novel complexes of institutions and associated ideas and behaviors" are: (1) competition, (2) science, (3) property rights, (4) medicine, (5) consumerism, and (6) the work ethic. He argues that the rest of the world now tries to adopt these killer apps to catch up to the development curve. Meanwhile, the developed markets in the West become complacent and fail to maintain these advantages. Even worse, some of these essential applications appear to have been corrupted and made economic growth unsustainable.

Another important factor contributes to the success and "God"-like authority of the market is the political consensus which we cannot take for granted. Based on the analyses of Rajan and Zingales (2003), the market economy is inherently unstable because the intrinsic creative-destructive forces are supposed to enhance the efficiency of the economy by effacing out the inefficient ones. These creative-destructive forces, which make the market economy so successful, could encounter meaningful resistance from both the incumbents vested interests and those being marginalized. On the one hand, they believed that the incumbents would attempt to stay in power by acquiring substantial competitive edges to the extent that competition in the market may not be longer viable. On the other hand, those being marginalized in the competition are deprived of their traditional safety net, so they may engage in political dissent and are incentivized to rally against the market through the political system to protect their interests.

What Is Wrong with the Market Economy: Human Values and Behaviors

In *The Great Transformation*, Polanyi (1944) criticizes how everything in this world becomes exchangeable commodities under the blanket of market economy. Even humanity is reduced to the source of labor and desires in the calculus of maximizing happiness. Loy (1997) concerns that the logic seems to be reversed in a way that human decisions can only be "rational" when supported by the right math. Our focus on consumption and profit, as driven by a fundamentally defective value-system of greed and delusion, seems to be justifiable even though it is manipulated by expensive advertising campaigns. Considering such a religious perspective of the market, the solution must also have a religious dimension. He explains that "this is a matter not of turning from secular to sacred values but of the need to discover how our secular obsessions have become symptomatic of a spiritual need that they cannot meet."

The Wealth of Nations (Smith 1843) is often quoted to justify human selfishness: "it is not from the benevolence of the butcher, the brewer, or the baker that we expect our dinner, but from their regard to their own interest. We address ourselves, not to their humanity but to their self-love." However, this understanding is "constrained, to the detriment of economics as a subject," according Sen (2010), without reference to the framework of *The Theory of Moral Sentiments* (Smith 1817) because the latter is crucial to appreciate that being rational is demanding. Human motivations are multifaceted, economics are intertwined with ethics the demands of rationality, and the codependent relationship with institu-

Fig. 3.1 Productivity as the economic force. Note: "Working hard at work today or working hard to find work tomorrow!" a slogan painted on the wall. (Source: Photo by author)

tions, and so forth. It also argues that human behaviors are motivated by more than self-interest, "humanity, justice, generosity, and public spirit, are the qualities most useful to others."—even though self-interest in the crude form of self-love or in the refined form of prudence "is most helpful to the individual" out of all virtues (Smith 1817) (Fig. 3.1).

Beyond selfishness or materials gain, economists have attempted to build economic models to address and explain behaviors in different aspects of life driven through a much richer set of values and preferences (Becker 1993). According to these models, individuals could maximize welfare in various forms, may they be selfish, altruistic, loyal, spiteful, or masochistic. Such a richer class of parameters is an extension of the traditional analysis of rational choice and an attempt to evaluate and anticipate individual choice as well as choices at a macro level. They reduce human decisions to economic analyses, ascribing functions of cost and preference to the problem, and suggest that decision-making would optimize these outcomes in the process. Instead of including other values such as justice, honor, relationship, and so forth in determining whether someone would commit a crime, engage in education or training, allocate resources to his or her next generations, and so forth, they believe that the criminal motives could be considered rationally as if they follow a consistent set of preferences.

Neoclassical economists have a difficult time understanding irrational behavior which deviates from the assumed rationality and self-interest during financial market meltdowns. Their theories appear to be inadequate theoretically and empirically to address the lack of predictability, stability, and sustainability of economic growth. Stiglitz (2014) criticizes the standard economic models which claim that in assumed well-functioning economies, an economic bubble (or crisis) does not exist. As a result, these models do not only fail to predict the occurrence and evolution of economic crises, they also fail to provide good policy guidance to respond and facilitate a recovery. Schumacher (1984) believes that when economists assume their theories have certain absolute, invariable, and universal truths, without any presuppositions—free from "metaphysics" or "values", they "suffer from a kind of metaphysical blindness".

Unlike other streams of science, the market economy as explained by economic theories seems to lack the constant, predictable relationships between inputs and outputs found in physics, biology or chemistry to explain human economic behaviors. At the market level, Stiglitz (2014) challenges the assumption that fundamental flaws in the standard model are only exposed during financial crises—crises are not the exceptional few cases where the standard model fails. In fact, he argues that the market economy was not even performing well before the crisis. He observed that the crisis in 2008 should not be viewed as an accident or shock from the outside but was "created, or at least enabled" by central banks. Most importantly, he believes that even when the standard model performs well in times of normal economic activity, the benefits produced when it is correct could not compensate for the losses resulted when it is wrong during the crisis. He points out that macroeconomics should particularly analyze and learn from these deep downturns if the research is genuinely concerned with overall societal welfare.

In economics, negative consequences not directly accounted for in a transaction, but borne by other third parties (society, future generations, the ecology, and so forth), are known as negative externalities. For example, the producer and consumer of robotics would not have considered the social cost of unemployment and re-training in their cost structures. On income disparity, the World Bank (2019) latest estimate, 736 million people in 2015 lived on less than US$1.9 a day—a widely recognized benchmark for defining the world's poor, down from 1.85 billion in 1990. With respect for the environment, it would be difficult for consumers to be aware of the enormous amount of water required for the entire production process of a cup of coffee—for example, 140 liters of water in the Netherlands (Chapagain and Hoekstra 2003).

At the individual level, our purchasing decisions in the consumer economy are often driven more by our desires than our needs. While we all have basic requirements to keep our body and mind nourished with food, clothing, and shelter, our desires for design, beauty, and quality are manifestations of self-gratification. Yet these objects of desire often appear on everyone's list of "must-haves." Some of us may have so many extra appliances, utensils, gadgets, items of clothing, and so on, that they are rarely used, even while the basic needs of the underprivileged members or our communities are not being met. It is indeed a paradox in our consumer economy that we appear to prefer more choices, but too much choice stresses us out (Schwartz 2004)—it is not only difficult to decide what to buy, it is also difficult to decide what to consume after we have made our impulsive purchases. The market economy indoctrinated consumer behaviors by advertisements, social norms, and peer pressure. It attempts to influence human decision on what make us happy—food, fame, power, education, healthcare, family, children, career, and so forth.

Efficiency in the market economy appears to equal maximum consumption with minimum amount of work, work hours, and even the "headcount" involved. Development seems to mean reducing work and work hours, instead of pursuing more meaningful and valuable work. In the *Small is Beautiful*, Schumacher (1984) suggested that, according to Buddhist teachings, work has its own meaning. From a Buddhist perspective, work should not be considered merely a means to satisfy our endless desires. Instead, it is an integral part of life, and a skill- and character-building process. Work, if conducted in accordance with the concept of right livelihood, is a practice of sustainable happiness.

As we outsource work, pushing away the problems and the undesirables, we are also outsourcing happiness. In addition to material consumption, social status and relationship such as achievements in education, property ownership, career, and family are elements for a happy life. Nonetheless, if human happiness is contingent on these achievements, it is arguable that human happiness is outsourced and outside of us. As much as it is difficult to outsource our suffering, it is also impossible to outsource our happiness. It is equally impossible to serve as the "contractor" for the happiness of other people. Even though we can cultivate the conditions leading to happiness, each of us is ultimately responsible for our own happiness.

While the market economy is an innovative mechanism for economic activities and is often time efficient, it has also brought forth substantial unintentional negative consequences. All the market participants together, for the sake of convenience, efficiency, utility, profit, and so forth, have fed an enormous giant market which in turn manipulate our preferences and desires, and enslaves us. In the process, income disparity has been widening, decisions become short-sighted, profit-oriented, and self-centered. According to WHO (2019), mental depression is now a common illness worldwide with more than 300 million people affected. It could have critical health impact to those affected including possible suicide with close to 800,000 people die due to suicide every year.

Chapter Summary

- Economics as a subject is an evolving field: it evolved from the discussion on household management to political economy, from wealth to well-being, behaviors, and choices.
- There are at least nine different schools of thought with different assumptions on individual ranging from Classical and Neoclassical schools to the Behaviorist.
- Broadly speaking, the subject could be defined by ten core principles from three perspectives of the individual decision-making, interaction among people, and the economy as a whole.
- Market economy could possibly be considered as a new religion with market being the new God based on consumerism as the core values, science as the theoretical bases, and economic activities (growth, production, and consumption) being the new path of salvation.

- Critics highlight that the market economy reduce to a defective value-system of greed and delusion manipulated by advertising.
- Hence, meaningful response to the "new religion of market" must also have a religious dimension.
- The seminal work of Smith posits that even though self-interest is the most helpful, there are other motivations and other important components essential to the functioning of the market economy.
- Beyond rationality and self-interest, economists also attempted to model and predict behaviors in different aspect of life driven by a much richer set of values and preferences.
- Fundamentally market economy, as explained by economic theories, seems to be lacking the constant predictable relationships between inputs and outputs found in physics, biology or chemistry.
- The standard economic model failed to explain past economic crises and they were not even performing well outside of the crises.
- Negative consequences were also not fully accounted for in economic transactions. There are substantial threats caused by economic activities at the individual, social, and environmental levels.

Study Questions

- How is economics evolved as a subject? And what are the changes in the underlying assumptions?
- What is wrong with rationality and self-interest being the core motivations of economy?
- Is the market economy stable or sustainable?
- Is the market predictable?
- What are the benefits and challenges of a market economy?

Suggested Essay Topics

- Economics as a subject—key schools of thought and developments
- Market economy as the new religion
- Beyond rationality and self-interest in economic model
- What is wrong with the market economy?
- Smith in *The Wealth of Nation* and *The Theory of Moral Sentiments*

Bibliography

Online Multimedia

IPCC. IPCC Special Report on Climate Change and Land. Intergovernmental Panel on Climate Change (IPCC). https://www.youtube.com/watch?v=LnBLrpJl6pY. Accessed 28 Sept 2019.

———. Special Report on the Ocean and Cryosphere in a Changing Climate. Intergovernmental Panel on Climate Change (IPCC). https://www.youtube.com/watch?v=CU3_NDklRVM. Accessed 28 Sept 2019.

———. IPCC Special Report on Global Warming of 1.5°C. Intergovernmental Panel on Climate Change (IPCC). https://www.youtube.com/watch?v=rVjp3TO_juI

Required Reading

Backhouse, Roger E., and Steven Medema. 2008. Economics, Definition of. In *The New Palgrave Dictionary of Economics*, ed. Steven N. Durlauf and Lawrence E. Blume, 720–722. New York: Palgrave Macmillan. Original edition, 1987.

Loy, David R. 1997. The Religion of the Market. *Journal of the American Academy of Religion* 65 (2): 275–290.

Smith, Adam. 1817. *The Theory of Moral Sentiments*. First American ed. Philadelphia: Anthony Finley.

Further Reading

Becker, Gary S. 1993. Nobel Lecture: The Economic Way of Looking at Behavior. *Journal of Political Economy* 101 (3): 385–409.

Chang, Ha-Joon. 2014. *Economics: The User's Guide*. London: Pelican, Penguin Books.

Chapagain, A. K., and A. Y. Hoekstra. 2003. The Water Needed to Have the Dutch Drink Coffee. UNESCO-IHE Institute for Water Education. http://waterfootprint.org/media/downloads/Report14.pdf. Accessed 1 Dec 2015.

Ferguson, Niall. 2011. *Civilization: The West and the Rest*. 1st ed. New York: Penguin Press.

Levitt, Steven D., and John A. List. 2008. Homo Economicus Evolves. *Science* 319 (5865): 909–910.

Mankiw, Gregory N. 2012. Ten Principles of Economics. In *Principles of Economics*, 6th ed., 1–17. Mason: South-Western Cengage Learning.

Marshall, Alfred. 1890. *Principal of Economics*. London: Macmillan. Reprint, 1949.

Mill, John S. 1967. Essays on Some Unsettled Questions of Political Economy. In *Collected Works of John Stuart Mill*, ed. J.M. Robson. Toronto: University of Toronto Press. Original edition, 1844.

Polanyi, Karl. 1944. *The Great Transformation: The Political and Economic Origins of Our Time.* Boston: Beacon Press.

Rajan, Raghuram, and Luigi Zingales. 2003. *Saving Capitalism from the Capitalists.* New York: Crown Business.

Robbins, Lionel C. 1935. *An Essay on the Nature and Significance of Economic Science.* 2nd ed. London: Macmillan. Original edition, 1932.

Salecl, Renata. 2010. *Choice.* London: Profile Books.

Samuelson, Paul A. 1967. *Economics.* 7th ed. New York: McGraw-Hill.

Schumacher, E. F. 1984. Buddhist Economics. In *Small Is Beautiful: Economics as if People Mattered.* London: Sphere Books. Original edition, 1973. http://www.centerforneweconomics.org/buddhist-economics

Smith, Adam. 1843. *An Inquiry into the Nature and Causes of the Wealth of Nations.* Edinburgh: Thomas Nelson.

Schwartz, Barry. 2004. *The Paradox of Choice: Why More Is Less.* New York: Ecco, HarperCollins Publishers.

Sen, Amartya. 2010. The Economist Manifesto. *New Statesman*, April 26, 29–30.

Steuart, James. 1767. *An Inquiry into the Principles of Political Economy.* London: A. Miller and T. Cadell.

Stiglitz, Joseph E. 2014. Reconstructing Macroeconomic Theory to Manage Economic Policy. In *Fruitful Economics*, ed. Eloi Laurent and Jacques Le Cacheux. New York: Palgrave Macmillan.

Tideman, Sander G. 2004. Gross National Happiness: Towards a New Paradigm in Economics. First International Conference on Operationalization of Gross National Happiness, Thimphu.

WHO. 2019. Depression—Key Facts. *World Health Organization.* https://www.who.int/news-room/fact-sheets/detail/depression. Accessed 11 Sept 2019.

World Bank. 2019. Understanding Poverty. *The World Bank.* http://www.worldbank.org/en/topic/poverty/overview. Accessed 11 Sept 2019.

PART III

The Cause

CHAPTER 4

Drivers Behind the Shortcomings of the Market Economy

Profit Maximization: Spirituality Versus Materiality

Friedman (1966) argued that a useful economic theory should be judged not by the descriptive realism of its assumption, but by its simplicity and fruitfulness as an engine of prediction. No doubt that the current market economy has received strong endorsement by policy makers, business leaders, and economists. It does not only challenge the relevance and usefulness of qualitative values in economic activities, but also imposes new materialistic values—of matter, things, and money.

To identify the drivers of the shortcomings of the market economy, the reason or motivation behind economic decisions are crucial. Among various motivations of decision-making in the market economy, Zsolnai (2011) looks into two significant ones being the principle of profit and the principle of rationality. He argues that the pursuit of profit as an economic reason, or as the principle of economic activities, has "two distinct but interrelated problems"—applying profit as the sole measure of rightness is the first problem, and upholding it as the main motivation of economic activities is the second one. Another shortcoming of a profit-driven mindset is the unfair bias toward the values of the strongest stakeholders and the lack of representation for other stakeholders in the market. For example, the preferences of natural beings and future generations will not be fully considered in current economic decisions. Interests of the poor and the disadvantaged with lower purchasing power are also under-represented.

E. C. H. Ng, *Introduction to Buddhist Economics*,
Studies in Buddhist Economics, Management, and Policy,
https://doi.org/10.1007/978-3-030-35114-4_4

This profit-driven mentality favors a self-centered and short-term preference of "here and now" and assumes all values can be reduced or commoditized into monetary values (Zsolnai 2011). Apart from profit consideration, other values outside of the market place are calculated with the same quantitative and market-based mechanism—everything seems to have a price and be traded—externalities can then be artificially "internalized" and the full cost associated with the activities be accounted for accordingly.

However, not everything can be expressed in monetary terms. For example, natural assets, human and social values such as ethics, aesthetics, health and safety cannot be easily expressed in monetary terms (Zsolnai 2011). Profit as the main motivation may crowd out intrinsic motivation and lead to increasing quantity but decreasing quality—agribusiness is an important case. It also cultivates self-centered value orientation, which according to Zsolnai (2011) could lead to socially insensitive and ethically irresponsible behaviors.

Despite Smith's elaborated discussions on virtues in *The Theory of Moral Sentiments*, the market seems to put more focus on self-interest and the invisible hand in *The Wealth of Nations*. Friedman (2002) suggested that social responsibility for a business corporation in a free market is to pursue profitability within the rules of the game. Objectivist ethics on the other hand, opposed the conventional notion of morality because the call for the greater and social goods seems to consistently sacrifice the best interests of the individual. Rand (1964) hold that "the actor must always be the beneficiary of his action and that man must act for his own rational self-interest." Nowadays, these views are being misinterpreted in the market economy as a sanction for amoral, irrational, and self-centered behaviors.

Economic Rationality: Consistency Versus Plurality of Human Motivations

Another key driver of economic activities in the market economy is rationality: the cognitive capacity of human beings to make logical, internally consistent (weak form) and self-interest maximizing (strong form) choices. Still, this "rational choice model" is very demanding on the cognitive capacity of human beings, who in reality have very limited information for decision-making. In real life, we make a sufficient approach to optimization, instead of maximizing ones—i.e. not the best but good enough choices with our bounded rationality (Simon 1955). Based on experiment data, Tversky and Kahneman (1974) make a similar criticism on the rational model and conclude that humans do not fully comply with the principle of rationality, and usually make myopic choices, which violates the principle of rationality.

Tversky, Kahneman, and Thaler together are the leading scholars in the Behavioral Economics which fundamentally challenge the rational assumptions of the Classical and Neoclassical schools of thought—that human behaviors can be explained by consistent, well-defined preferences, and rational choices. Their empirical studies demonstrated that anomalies to rational assumptions of human behaviors and psychology are in fact quite common—hence an alternative set of principles or assumptions are required the describe or even predict human behaviors. Among these anomalies, endowment effect, loss aversion, and status quo bias are a few robust cases which demonstrate systematic deviations of human behaviors and psychology from the principle of rationality (Kahneman et al. 1991). Thaler (1988) also illustrated in the "ultimatum game" that humans could make decisions on values such as fairness, which is also contingent on social consensus on appropriate behaviors, beyond rational utility-maximizing reasoning.

Sen (2004) criticizes both the weak form and strong form of rationality. He illustrates that internal consistency cannot be a guarantee of a person's rationality because it does not reflect the complex motivations of agents in their economic affairs (duty, loyalty, and goodwill in addition to self-interest). The rational choice model covers only the "language module" on the left hemisphere of the human brain—many other considerations are not covered in human decision-making. For example, Mansbridge (1995) has developed a tripartite scheme of human motivation including duty, self-interest, and love as the irreducible motives of human behaviors. Hume (1911) has also argued for a rich variety of human motivations including principle, interest, and affection.

Zsolnai (2011) proposes that economic activities can be claimed reasonable only if they satisfy the test of ecology, future generations, and society. On ecology, he echoes Aldo Leopold's arguments in *A Sand County Almanac* that "a thing is right when it tends to preserve the integrity, stability, and beauty of the biotic community. It is wrong when it tends otherwise" (Leopold 1948). On future generations, Zsolnai believes that the freedom of future generations can only be reassured by meeting the principles proposed by Weiss (1989): (i) conservation of options; (ii) conservation of quality; and (iii) conservation of access. On society, an important perspective to evaluate human well-being is the concept of capabilities proposed by Sen (1992). Capability is a reflection of the freedom of a person to achieve valuable functioning. Therefore, it can be interpreted as substantive freedom that people enjoy.

Fig. 4.1 Hong Kong: The free market economy. Note: Hong Kong could serve as a good case study of the interaction between money and morality. (Source: Photo by author)

Accordingly, Zsolnai (2011) believes that the main goal of economic activities should not be profit-making but providing the right livelihood for those who are involved. If economic activities can meet the test of ecology, future generations and society, profit may or may not follow but the richness of human beings and the quality of life can be attained (Fig. 4.1).

Moral Disengagement: Relevancy of Ethics and Values

While markets are extremely effective and efficient in generating information and facilitating resource allocation, research demonstrates that markets display a tendency towards eroding moral standards in the context of individual decision-making, in a way that market interaction causally affects the willingness to accept severe, negative consequences for a third party

(Falk and Szech 2013). It could be explained by three significant features of market interactions. Firstly, responsibility and a sense of guilt may appear to be shared and thus diminished in a transaction where more than one party is involved; secondly, prevailing norms revealed in market interactions suggest that certain self-interest based behaviors are "ethically" or "socially" permissible simply because others in the market place are doing the same. Finally, markets divert decision-making from other possible qualitative adverse consequences and the moral implications of the transactions because economic activities put so much focus on the materialistic aspects. In the market place, there is a common "replacement" logic where participants might think "if I don't buy or sell, someone else will" (Falk and Szech 2013). Market participants conclude that appealing to morality can only address the negative market externalities to a limited extent.

In addition to a profit-driven mindset, market mechanism can lead to deteriorating moral sentiments by facilitating the mechanisms of moral disengagement. Human beings conduct psychosocial maneuvering by which moral self-sanctions become disengaged, permitting oneself a variety of misbehaviors without carrying any moral concern. According to Bandura (1990), self-sanctions can be disengaged by: (1) reconstructing the conduct, (2) obscuring personal causal agency, (3) misrepresenting or disregarding the injurious consequences of one's actions, and (4) vilifying the recipients of maltreatment by blaming and devaluating them. In practice, research reveal that when people are more concerned with their self-enhancement goals, the more they are likely to resort to moral disengaging mechanisms with respect to their civic duties and obligations, justifying transgressions when their self-interest is at stake by (Caprara and Capanna 2006). Similarly, for market economy followers who are concerned with their self-interest and believe in the natural order of the "Invisible Hand" of the market, they are more likely to deploy moral disengagement mechanisms which will do more harm to others (Zsolnai 2011).

Cohn et al. (2014) showed in their research an alarming case that the identity of being bank employees, once revealed as such, seemed to be correlated with a higher level of dishonesty in comparison to other professions. The same bank employees did not show a higher level of dishonesty if their identity as bank employees was not brought to the attention of the experiment subjects. Their results suggest that the prevailing business culture in the banking industry may favor dishonest behaviors, leading to a loss of reputation and jeopardize the trust and stability of the financial industry as a whole.

If we look at the core reasons why the market economy is unsustainable, greed (Pāli: *lobha*), aversion (Pāli: *dosa*), delusion (Pāli: *moha*) at the individual and societal level contribute to many faulty and irrational decisions. With Buddhist Threefold Training in moral discipline (Pāli: *silā*), mental concentration (Pāli: *samādhi*) and wisdom (Pāli: *paññā*), specific changes are possible. As this book further discusses later, the Threefold Training can be integrated into daily life so that we can live in a Buddhist Economy with sustainable economic development. We can change the world starting with ourselves today.

Limits of Markets: What Is Not for Sale?

Even though the markets have shortcomings as driven by the principle of profit and rationality, they have many benefits in economic functions and even contribute to moral values such as trust and cooperativeness. Other non-market-driven mechanisms are not flawless and have other poor track records (Falk and Szech 2013). The question is therefore how the markets should be applied, should there be a limit to the market operations, beyond which the benefits cannot be justified the moral, political, social, and ecological costs involved.

Indeed, markets and market-oriented thinking have extended to spheres of life previously untouched by the markets. Sandel (1998) studied the interaction between the market economy and society and found examples, such as the commodification of books, the privatization of prisons, the commercialization of governments and universities. He concluded that this tendency of market-oriented thinking is "by and large a bad thing, a development that should be resisted" because the markets change the character of the subject items involved. He argues for some moral limits of markets distinguishing where the markets belong and where they do not. This distinction requires all of us to reflect on the meaning and purpose, and the values of the subjects involved (Sandel 2012). His core inquiry is: "Are there some things that should not be bought and sold, and, if so, why?" (Sandel 2005).

Sandel (2005) argues that there are two reasons namely, corruption and coercion, to consider a limit to market operations. By corruption he means that when a certain good is bought or sold in a monetary exchange, it becomes spoilt or degraded, corrupted or diminished in value, e.g. some moral and civic goods. This objection is not necessarily to the markets per se, but to its operations, i.e. whether the background conditions of the trade is fair or just, whether it is acceptable to trade and put a market value on the goods involved. The problem cannot be addressed by fixing the background conditions and applies under conditions of equality and inequality alike. In other words, trading or putting a price on the activity or object is fundamentally unjust. It would erode the morality of the individual or society involved. In contrast to the market mechanisms, which only focus on a consensual price, a qualitative judgment should be involved in the intrinsic worth and the character of the thing. While Utilitarianism, notably Benthamite Utilitarianism, would argue that all goods are commensurable, i.e. could be translated or reduced without loss into a common unit of measurement—price or money—this objection to corruption suggests otherwise (Sandel 1998).

Even though market is a valuable and effective tool for organizing productive activity, Sandel (2012) is particularly concerned about the influences which market mechanisms have on our daily lives, and which have turned our society into a market society. A market society is a society where market values become inseparable from every aspect our human decision-making, every social relationship become a transaction. It may change the meaning or value of goods being exchanged, particularly for non-material goods and social practices such as education and civic life. On one hand, human beings should not be "bought and sold" like "commodities" because humans should be worthy of respect (Sandel 2010). On the other hand, the very meaning of civic society may change when certain civic or public activities, such as military service, voting and distribution adopt market mechanisms (Sandel 1998, 2005, 2010).

Instead of a market society, Sandel calls for a republican society which freedom is not narrowly defined by self-interest, but by the freedom "to participate in shaping the forces that govern the collective destiny" (Sandel 1998). This republican conception of citizenship would require and seek its citizens to develop a fuller range of virtues, beyond the liberal concept of toleration and respect. It includes "a moral bond with the community whose fate is at stake, a sense of obligation for one's fellow citizens, a willingness to sacrifice individual interests for the sake of the common good, and the ability to deliberate well about common purposes and ends" (Sandel 1998). This conception also contrasts with the liberal concept which emphasizes respect for the rights of individual and tolerance, or the pluralist concept which emphasizes individual's freedom to identify their interests and vote accordingly. He suggests that the foundation of this republican theory could be one of a modest form, which takes civic virtues instrumentally, i.e. these virtues make a political society possible for each citizen to maintain their right to choose and achieve their goals.

Another more robust form considers these civic virtues as an essential part of a good life. It is not the means but the ends of a citizen's life. Participation in politics or public services would then require and cultivate human faculties that other activities could not achieve. Sandel (1998) argues that according to the republican concept of citizenship, the "public realm is not only a place of common provision but also a setting of civic education." Our experience in functioning as a citizen will be quite different if we approach our life as a citizen based on market economic interests or civic virtues. Taking military service as an example, he argues that the coercion argument would object to market mechanisms and the use of economic calculations because the choice of joining the military service may be affected or reflect deep inequalities in life. On the other hand, the moral corruption argument would suggest that military service should not be taken as just another job. Rousseau (2003) discussed in *The Social Contract* how the meaning of citizenship and the duties of public service had been corrupted by money:

> In a country that is truly free, the citizens do everything with their own arms and nothing by means of money; so far from paying to be exempted their duties, they would even pay for the privilege of fulfilling them themselves.

The same argument would apply to the influence of money to voting decisions and distribution. In a society with too much inequality, that the fairness of agreements people make could be undermined. People are not truly free in choosing their jobs at their preferred wage. They are no longer "truly free to choose and pursue their values and ends" (Sandel 1998). Accordingly, freedom is not merely expressed through the possession of primary goods but through capabilities like the "expression of freedoms" to "choose between different ways of living" (Sen 2003). Smith (1843) agreed with this notion as he believed that human beings are essentially similar irrespective of class, gender, race or nationality with equal potential. He argued that "the difference of natural talents in different men … seems to arise not so much from nature, as from habit, custom and education."

On the other hand, coercion means that people may be forced to buy or sell things involuntarily because of severe inequality or dire economic necessity (Sandel 2005). To know whether a good should be traded is different from knowing its price. It is a qualitative, instead of quantitative, judgment to access what mode of valuation is appropriate. Sandel (2005) argues against those libertarian philosophers and laissez-faire economists who believe that freedom consists of voluntary exchanges in the market economy despite intrinsic inequality. Even when our society becomes fairer where people can make free, rather than coerced, choices, he believes that it is critical to beware of the process of commodification. There are still dimensions of life which go beyond consent, moral and civic goods that markets do not honor and money cannot buy.

Can We Buy Well-Being and Happiness?

If there are moral limits to the markets, what is the relationship between the markets and human well-being and happiness? To answer this question, it is important to first define the meaning of happiness which have evolved significantly over human history. Ims (2013) argues that happiness, in a deep sense, is "activity based" and strongly related to "self-realization and other-orientation"—it is more an inner development of the individual than an external environmental factor. In this sense, happiness is a subjective, experienced form of human wellness. Therefore, his research concluded that "money does not make people happy, but people make people happy."

Veenhoven (2000) distinguishes between different qualities of life which could be broadly presented through a two-by-two matrix with outer and inner qualities on the one side, and life chances and life results on the other. On the one hand, outer qualities, when intersect with life chances and life results, respectively, will determine liveability of the environment and utility of life. On the other hand, inner qualities, when intersect with life chances and life results, respectively, will determine life-ability of person and appreciation of life. In other words, while external environment affects the "habitability" of the environment and hence our welfare, our inner qualities affect how much we can live the most out of our potentials and capabilities and make life meaningful or useful—subjectively how happy or satisfied we are with our life.

According to "Deep Ecology" philosophy, organisms are knots in a field of intrinsic relations. Self-realization of all beings—not only for man—is the central aim. Self-realization for humans cannot be obtained unless we take into consideration other sentient beings' self-realization (Ims 2013). The essence of Deep Ecology thinking can be summed up by the motto of Naess (1989): "Live a rich life with simple means." However, the most common measurement of human wellness in the market economy is through the level of economic activity (Gross Domestic Product, "GDP"). Hence material production, consumption, and possession are considered instrument of happiness and more is better. This "welfare" approach is a materialistic and economic description of human wellness (Ims 2013). Rising income will increase means and opportunities, but research suggests that it may have little lasting effect on well-being (Easterlin 2003). Within a given country, the Easterlin (1995) Paradox suggested that economic growth as measured by real income or GDP per capita did not seem to associate with an increase in reported well-being. If relative income remains stable while the absolute level of income in a given country increases, individual well-being may not change. According to the hedonic adaption, people also want more when the happiness generated by material things wears off: (1) rising aspirations motivate people to accomplish more and more; (2) wants are unquenchable: "the more one acquires, the more one wants"; (3) people expect to be happier in the future than in the past (Frey 2008).

According to Ims (2013), a welfare approach of measuring human happiness through GDP is also misleading because (1) it does not consider the impact of income inequality; (2) it assumes that we can only observe how people behave but not how they really feel; (3) externalities are not accounted for. It also neglects the damages and depletion of environment resources. As Robert Kennedy (1968) remarked, the Gross National Product ("GNP") "measures everything in short, except that which makes life worthwhile."

Even though GNP measures the productivity for the economy in aggregate, it does not measure happiness (Ims 2013). Higher income is not the only decisive factor for happiness (Frey 2008). In addition to basic material needs, well-being needs to be anchored in strengths and virtues, which in turn must be seen through a higher ideal: "Just as the good life is something beyond the pleasant life, the meaningful life is beyond the good life" (Seligman 2002). More importantly, even if a gross national measurement may reflect certain level of aggregate happiness, focusing on "the greatest happiness of the greatest number" may violate single individual rights in favor of the common good. It is because this utilitarian reasoning is built upon three axioms: (1) consequentialism, (2) welfarism and (3) sum-ranking with no attention to inequalities. Moral value under utilitarian consideration is justified based upon the effects that follow the actions. In other words, not only is GNP a poor measurement of aggregate happiness, it is an even less adequate measurement of individual well-being and happiness.

Chapter Summary

- Current market economic model has not only crowded out some qualitative values but has also imposed new materialistic values of matter, things, and money.
- To identify the drivers of the shortcomings of the market economy, the reason or motivation behind economic decisions are crucial. The principle of profit and the principle of rationality are two significant ones.
- The problem is not the pursuit of profit but using profit as the sole measure of rightness and main motivation.
- This principle of profit also has an unfair bias towards the values of the strongest stakeholders, favor a short-term orientation of here and now with only quantitative, market-based considerations.
- The principle of rationality worships rationality in human decision-making but scholars in the Behavioral Economics fundamentally challenge the rational assumptions of human behaviors and psychology.
- Humans have a wide range of motivations. Zsolnai proposes that economic activities should satisfy the test of ecology, future generation, and society.
- Market mechanism displays a tendency toward eroding moral standards in individual decision-making as explained by the process of moral disengagement and self-sanctions: (1) reconstructing the conduct, (2) obscuring personal causal agency, (3) misrepresenting or disregarding the injurious consequences of one's actions, and (4) vilifying the recipients of maltreatment by blaming and devaluating them.
- There should be some moral limits of markets for both corruption and coercion considerations. The markets change the character of the subject items involved.
- Corruption means when a certain good is bought or sold, it becomes spoilt or degraded, corrupted or diminished in value; coercion means that people may be forced to buy or sell things involuntarily because of severe inequality or dire economic necessity.
- There are many different meanings of happiness. Material well-being is fundamental but true happiness may call for self-realization and the realization of others.
- Gross National Product is a measure for quantitative and material affluency but it does not measure a full range of values that contribute to individual well-being and happiness.

Study Questions

- What are the core causes behind the shortcomings of the markets?
- What is the principle of profit and principle of rationality? What is wrong with these principles?
- What are the criteria for responsible decision making?
- Why are values relevant to economic decisions?
- Does the market make us immoral?
- Does money make us happy?
- What is the relationship between welfare and well-being?

Suggested Essay Topics

- Moral limits of the markets
- Moral and material values in the context of market economy
- The core causes behind the shortcomings of the markets
- Principle of profit and its impact to the market economy
- Principle of rationality and its implications to economic decision making
- Moral disengagement and case study
- From welfare to well-being

Bibliography

Online Multimedia

de Botton, Alain. 2016. The Dawn of Capitalism. *The School of Life*. Last modified 4 January 2016. https://www.youtube.com/watch?v=Yh_hRS15n_8&index=15&list=PLwxNMb28XmpehnfQOa4c0E7j3GIj4qFEj

Required Reading

Loy, David R. 1997. The Religion of the Market. *Journal of the American Academy of Religion* 65 (2): 275–290.

Sandel, Michael J. 2005. Markets, Morals, and Civic Life. *Bulletin of the American Academy of Arts and Sciences* 58 (Summer): 6–10.

Smith, Adam. 1817. *The Theory of Moral Sentiments*. First American ed. Philadelphia: Anthony Finley.

Zsolnai, László. 2011. Redefining Economic Reason. In *Spiritual Humanism and Economic Wisdom: Essays in Honour of Luk Bouchaert's 70th Anniversary*, ed. Hendrik Opdebeeck and László Zsolnai, 187–201. Antwerpen & Apeldoom: Garant Publishers.

Further Reading

Bandura, Albert. 1990. Mechanisms of Moral Disengagement. In *Origins of Terrorism: Psychologies, Ideologies, Theologies, and State of Mind*, ed. Walter Reich, 161–191. Cambridge: Cambridge University Press.

Caprara, Gian, and Cristina Capanna. 2006. Moral Disengagement in the Exercise of Civic-ness. In *Interdisciplinary Yearbook of Business Ethics 2006*, 87–98. Oxford: Peter Lang Publishers.

Cohn, Alain, Ernst Fehr, and Michel A. Maréchal. 2014. Business Culture and Dishonesty in the Banking Industry. *Nature* 516 (7529): 86–89.

Easterlin, Richard A. 1995. Will Raising the Incomes of all Increase the Happiness of All? *Journal of Economic Behavior & Organization* 27 (1995): 35–47.

———. 2003. Building a Better Theory of Well-Being. IZA Discussion Paper Series 742 (March).

Falk, Armin, and Nora Szech. 2013. Morals and Markets. *Science* 340: 707–711.

Frey, Bruno. 2008. *Happiness. A Revolution in Economics*. Cambridge: The MIT Press.

Friedman, Milton. 1966. The Methodology of Positive Economics. In *The Methodology of Positive Economics*. Chicago: University of Chicago.

———. 2002. *Capitalism and Freedom*. Chicago: University of Chicago Press. Original edition, 1962.

Hume, David. 1911. In *A Treatise of Human Nature II*, ed. T.H. Green and T.H. Grose. London: Everyman Library.

Ims, Knut J. 2013. From Welfare to Well-Being and Happiness. In *Handbook of Business Ethics*, ed. László Zsolnai, 217–248. Bern: Peter Lang.

Kahneman, Daniel, Jack L. Knetsch, and Richard H. Thaler. 1991. Anomalies: The Endowment Effect, Loss Aversion, and Status Quo Bias. *Journal of Economic Perspectives* 5 (1): 193–206.

Kennedy, Robert. (1968). Remarks at the University of Kansas (on March 18, 1968). John F. Kennedy Presidential Library and Museum. Accessed 1 Sept 2019. https://www.jfklibrary.org/learn/about-jfk/the-kennedy-family/robert-f-kennedy/robert-f-kennedy-speeches/remarks-at-the-university-of-kansas-march-18-1968

Leopold, Aldo. 1948. *A Sand County Almanac*. Oxford: Oxford University Press.

Mansbridge, Jane. 1995. Rational Choice Gains by Losing. *Political Psychology* 16 (1): 137–155.

Naess, Arne. 1989. *Ecology, Community and Lifestyle*. Translated and edited by David Rothenberg. Cambridge: Cambridge University Press.

Rand, Ayn. 1964. *The Virtue of Selfishness*. New York: New American Library.

Rousseau, Jean 2003. *On the Social Contract*. Trans. G. D. H. Cole. New York: Dover Publications. Original edition, On the Social Contract or Principles of Political Right, 1913, London: J. M. Dent.

Sandel, Michael J. 1998. *What Money Can't Buy: The Moral Limits of Markets*. Tanner Lectures on Human Values, Brasenose College, Oxford, May 11 and 12, 1998.

———. 2010. *Justice: What's the Right Thing to Do?* New York: Farrar, Straus and Giroux.

———. 2012. *What Money Can't Buy: The Moral Limits of Markets*. New York: Farrar, Straus and Giroux.

Seligman, Martin. 2002. *Authentic Happiness. Using the New Positive Psychology to Realize Your Potential for Lasting Fulfillment*. New York: Free Press.

Sen, Amartya. 1992. *Inequality Reexamined*. New York: Russell Sage Foundation.

———. 2003. Development as Capability Expansion. In *Readings in Human Development: Concepts Measures and Policies for a Development Paradigm*, ed. Sakiko Fukuda-Parr and Shiva A.K. Kumar, 41–58. New Delhi: Oxford University Press.

———. 2004. *Rationality and Freedom*. Cambridge: Harvard University Press.

Simon, Herbert A. 1955. A Behavioral Model of Rational Choice. *The Quarterly Journal of Economics* 69 (1): 99–118.

Smith, Adam. 1843. *An Inquiry into the Nature and Causes of the Wealth of Nations*. Edinburgh: Thomas Nelson.

Thaler, Richard. 1988. Anomalies: The Ultimate Game. *Journal of Economic Perspectives* 2 (4): 195–206.

Tversky, Amos, and Daniel Kahneman. 1974. Judgment Under Uncertainty: Heuristics and Biases. *Science* 185 (4157): 1124–1131.

Veenhoven, Ruut. 2000. The Four Qualities of Life: Ordering Concepts and Measures of the Good Life. *Journal of Happiness Studies* 1 (1): 1–39.

Weiss, Edith. 1989. *In Fairness to Future Generations: International Law, Common Patrimony, and Intergeneration Equity*. Tokyo: The United Nations University Press.

PART IV

The Cessation

CHAPTER 5

Buddhist Economics Theory

Pursuit of Happiness in Market and in Buddhism

The *Buddha* says that all living beings desire happiness and recoil from suffering (even spiritual eternalism and annihilationist materialism are arguably sharing the same desire). The difference, however, is that true happiness means something very different in Buddhism than it does to other philosophies. The *Buddha* says, "What others call happiness, that the Noble Ones declare to be suffering. What others call suffering, that the Noble Ones have found to be happiness" (Sn 3.12). Happiness by the world means those perceptions and conceptions which are "agreeable, pleasant and charming" and unsatisfactory when they cease. But the Noble Ones consider the cessation of all these attachments and self-existence true happiness.

As a religious teacher, the *Buddha* never praised poverty. In fact, the *Buddha* singled out hunger to be "the worst disease" and poverty to be the most socially destabilizing factor. However, even if a person is very rich, in the presence of another who is richer, he will feel poor by comparison. In the *Sabbāsava Sutta* (All the Taints), the *Buddha* says, "the destruction of the taints is for one who knows and sees, not for one who does not know and see" (MLDB. MN 2). The *Buddha* taught that the cessation of suffering requires one to know and see. It requires us to know and see the truth about the real nature of our "self" and our experienced world, which is, according to the Buddhist teachings, impermanence, unsatisfactoriness or suffering, and non-self. On the other hand, the wrong view of self will

E. C. H. Ng, *Introduction to Buddhist Economics*,
Studies in Buddhist Economics, Management, and Policy,
https://doi.org/10.1007/978-3-030-35114-4_5

Fig. 5.1 The stone of wisdom. Note: The stone of wisdom at Alpbach, Austria. (Source: Photo by author)

keep us bound, "not freed from birth, ageing, and death, from sorrow, lamentation, pain, grief, and despair" (MLDB. MN 2) (Fig. 5.1).

Karunadasa (2015) illustrates that in Buddhism there is an inseparable causal correlation between morality and happiness. Essentially, what is morally good leads to happiness and what is morally bad leads to unhappiness. The Buddhist term for what is morally good is "skillful" (Pāli: *kusala*) and morally bad is "unskillful" (Pāli: *akusala*). A mind which is poisoned with the three poisons of greed, hatred, and ignorance, is a mind that is "unskillful" (morally bad); a mind that is "defiled", a mind that is "ill", a mind that is "in bondage"—a mind that "suffers". In contrast, a mind that is free from the three poisons is a mind that is "skillful" (morally good), "pure", "well", and "in freedom"–in other words, a mind that is "happy". One option is to change the nature of the world to conform to our desires. The other option is to change our behaviors to be in harmony with the nature of the world. This book further discusses the Buddhist theory of moral life in the Chap. 6.

According to the *Buddha*, it is only when we have our mind under our own control that we can be truly happy, not when we come under the control of our own mind (Karunadasa 2015). To keep our mind under control, we should develop mindfulness (Pāli: *sati*) and clear comprehension (Pāli: *sampajañña*). To be mindful is not the same as being self-conscious. When we are self-conscious, we are obsessed with ourselves; we tend to react to situations thoughtlessly instead of responding to them after careful reflection. Greed, hatred, and ignorance are the three poisons that corrode our mental and physical health and prevent us from true happiness.

The *Buddha* draws our attention to many levels of happiness, ranging from the lowest to the highest, from the grossest to the most refined. Since there are many levels of happiness, the *Buddha* asks his disciples to make a "proper evaluation of happiness" (Pāli: *sukha-vinicchaya*). The purpose of this evaluation is to sacrifice lower levels of happiness in order to pursue higher levels of happiness (Karunadasa 2015). It is this psychological resistance that prevents humans from pursuing higher levels of non-sensuous happiness. Such happiness, the *Buddha* says, should not be feared (Pāli: *na bhāyitabbaṃ*). Immediately after his realization, this occurred to the *Buddha*-to-be: "Why am I afraid of that happiness that has nothing to do with sensual pleasure and unwholesome states?" Therefore, the Buddhist path to highest happiness is certainly not through suffering, neither does it involve vexation, despair and anguish. Reaching a higher level of freedom from suffering and pressure takes effort. We are responsible for our happiness as much as we are responsible for our moral actions.

The *Buddha* describes the Noble Eightfold Path as the path "to be trodden with Joy (Pāli: *pīti-gamanīyo*)." He also reminds us that "it is only when one does not give up happiness which accords with the *Dhamma* that the effort will be fruitful." This shows the indispensability of happiness in order to pursue higher levels of happiness. It is certainly not through suffering, but through happiness, that the *Buddha* penetrated the Truth of Suffering (CDB. SN 56.35):

> … I do not say that the breakthrough to the Four Noble Truths is accompanied by suffering or displeasure. Rather the breakthrough to the Four Noble Truths is accompanied only by happiness and joy.

The ultimate goal of Buddhism is the cessation of suffering: "both formerly and now also I proclaim two things: suffering and the cessation of suffering." Cessation of suffering is another expression for happiness and "[it] is the only thing we pursue for its own sake" (Karunadasa 2015). In the Buddhist teachings, the mechanism of human psychology and, more fundamentally, the origination of human suffering—and hence the mechanism of human mental as well as life evolution—is expounded in the twelve-factored formulation of dependent arising. Although the twelve-factored formulation is presented sequentially, it is important to appreciate that these factors arise together. As important as ignorance is as a root cause, it is not the first cause. All twelve factors co-arise dependently and lead us into this mundane order of endless suffering. In order to break this mundane spiral and deliver real change away from the inertia of our thought processes, we must be capable of transcending this mundane order with the transcendental order of dependent arising.

Box 5.1 Upanisa Sutta: The Discourse on Supporting Conditions (CDB. SN 12.23)[1]

The Mundane Order of Dependent Arising: With ignorance (Pāli: *avijja*) as condition, volitional formations (Pāli: *sankhara*); with volitional formations as condition, consciousness (Pāli: *viññana*); with consciousness as condition, name-and-form (Pāli: *namarupa*); with name-and-form as condition, six sense bases (Pāli: *saḷāyatana*); with six sense bases as condition, contact (Pāli: *phassa*); with contact as condition, feeling (Pāli: *vedana*); with feeling as condition, craving (Pāli: *tanha*), with craving as condition, clinging (Pāli: *upādāna*); with clinging as condition, existence (*bhava*); with existence as condition, birth (Pāli: *jati*); with birth as condition, suffering (Pāli: *dukkha*) …

The Transcendental Order of Dependent Arising: With suffering (*dukkha*) as condition, faith (Pāli: *saddhā*); with faith as condition, gladness (Pāli: *pāmojja*); with gladness as condition, rapture (Pāli: *pīti*); with rapture as condition, tranquility (Pāli: *passaddhi*); with tranquility as condition, happiness (Pāli: *sukha*); with happiness as condition, concentration (Pāli: *samādhi*); with concentration as condition, knowledge and vision of things as they really are (Pāli: *yathā bhūtañāṇadassana*); with knowledge and vision of things as they really are as condition, revulsion (Pāli: *nibbida*); with revulsion as condition, dispassion (Pāli: *viraga*); with dispassion as condition, liberation (Pāli: *vimutti*); with liberation as condition, knowledge of destruction (Pāli: *āsavakkhaye ñaṇa*).

[1] See Bodhi (2013) for further reference.

In the quest for the highest happiness, the decisive turning point is not fear but a real encounter with suffering. From then onward, the sequence is not one of suffering, but degrees of happiness leading to the highest happiness. This idea is clearly explained in the "transcendental depending arising" or "a dependent arising that leads to the transcendence of the world." Happiness can also achieved through the Four Sublime States or Divine Abodes (Pāli: ***Brahmavihāra***): (a) loving kindness (Pāli: ***mettā***): love, without the desire to possess; (b) compassion (Pāli: ***karunā***): compassion to all suffering living beings; (c) altruistic joy (Pāli: ***muditā***): the ability to feel happy and joyful at the success of another; (d) equanimity (Pāli: ***upekkhā***): the perfect, unshakable balance of mind (Karunadasa 2015).

Although happiness is a state of mind, there is no easy "on" or "off" switch. To see the present moment as a wonderful moment, to see happiness in the here and now, we need to uproot our entrenched thoughts and our tendency to grasp, as well as our fixation on the past and the future. Pursuing sustainable happiness through the Noble Eightfold Path takes time, effort, and patience—but it is worth it. Relying on worldly consumptions is not sustainable because they—as well as our perceptions toward them—are intrinsically impermanent. To protect ourselves from the emotional roller coaster which we cannot rely on, we need to develop a better understanding of ourselves and our external world, and what brings us sustainable happiness (Table 5.1).

Table 5.1 Happiness in market and in Buddhism

Happiness in market	*Happiness in Buddhism*
Proliferation of self-identity	Cessation of self
Proliferation of perceptions	Cessation of attachment to perceptions
Proliferation of conceptions, ideas, etc.	Cessation of views
Paradox of choices	Focus
Ignorance of impermanence	Insight to the true nature
Immoral indulgence of desires, sensual pleasure	Moral ways of living, spiritual
Unskillful and unwholesome states	Skillful and wholesome states
Mind is not pure, defiled	Mind is pure, undefiled
Not mindful, mind in bondage	Mindful, mind is truly free
Not under the control of our own mind	Under the control of our own mind
Mainly material satisfaction(unbalanced life)	Beyond material satisfaction (balanced life)

Source: Author with reference to Bodhi (2013) and Gethin (1998)

What Makes Buddhist Economics "Buddhist"?

Buddhist Economics is "Buddhist" because it is consistent with the teachings of the *Buddha*. This section summarizes some of the core principles which are further analyzed in the rest of the book. In the *Dhammacakkappavattana Sutta* (CDB. SN 56.11), the initial teachings of the *Buddha* comprise (1) the Middle Way transcending above the two extremes of the pursuit of happiness in sensual pleasures and the pursuit of self-mortification; (2) the Noble Eightfold Path, and (3) the Four Noble Truths. As discussed in the Chap. 2, the Noble Eightfold Path could also be understood from the framework of the Threefold Training of moral discipline, mental concentration, and wisdom which are briefly discussed herein but will be further looked into the next few chapters.

Buddhist Economics should therefore also adhere to the moral discipline which is core to the Buddhist world-view. To serve our best self-interest, Buddhist Economics advocates a life based on moral discipline. When our mind and body are not deluded, we can achieve sustainable happiness and freedom. The second important component of Buddhist Economics is the training of mental concentration which could be interpreted as how humans pay the right attention on the right objects that bring wisdom. Finally, Buddhist Economics is Buddhist because of the Buddhist wisdom of selflessness (Pāli: *anatta*) and dependent arising (Pāli: *paṭiccasamuppāda*). While the market economy focuses on an individual self as the operating entity, the Buddhist teachings on selflessness and dependent arising posit that there is no real self-entity independent of other conditions. Our happiness and well-being are inseparable from those of our past, present, and future generations, our natural environment, and rest of the ecosystem. We cannot survive and operate in a vacuum.

Hence Buddhist Economics is also unique in its understanding of the world, how we pay attention, and how to implement changes at the individual, societal, and environmental levels. Buddhist teachings have in-depth analyses on the subject of "view" and how view affects our decision-making and actions. The *One Thing Sutta* (Pāli: *Ekadhamma Sutta*) explains that wrong view is like a bitter cucumber seed being planted in moist soil; all the nutrients from the soil and water will only contribute to the fruition of a bitter cucumber because that is the nature of the seed itself:

> … for a person of wrong view, whatever bodily, verbal, or mental kamma he instigates and undertakes in accordance with that view, and whatever his volition, yearning, inclination, and volitional activities, all lead to what is unwished for, undesired, and disagreeable, to harm and suffering. For what reason? Because the view is bad. (CDB. AN 1.314)

From the Buddhist perspective, wrong view is the root cause of human suffering. The *Buddha* taught on the one hand that wrong view explains why "unarisen unwholesome qualities arise and arisen unwholesome qualities increase and expand" (NDB. AN 1.306). On the other hand, it also accounts for why our "unarisen wholesome qualities do not arise and arisen wholesome qualities decline" (NDB. AN 1.308). It also leads to our being "reborn in the plane of misery, in a bad destination, in the lower world, in hell" (NDB. AN 1.312).

A well-known story in the *Tittha Sutta* (Ud 6.4) depicts how, in the search for reality, we think and act like a blind person trying to describe an elephant with access to only a small part of the whole. We tend to claim certainty when we only see the tip of the iceberg. According to Buddhist teachings, intellect is one of the six sense bases (along with eyes, ears, nose, tongue, and body), which operate in conditioned and interdependent ways. In *The Ball of Honey Sutra* (MLDB. MN 18) (*Madhupiṇḍika Sutta*), the *Buddha* teaches in great detail the interaction between intellect, ideas, and intellect-consciousness, and how we are bound by our ideas. In other words, our ideas and views are conditioned by our feelings, perceptions, and so forth. Our views are not necessarily a direct reflection of objective truths or realities. Regardless of whether the views and ideologies are true or false, Karunadasa (2015) argues that Buddhist teaching considers that "dogmatic attachment … is very much more detrimental and fraught with more danger than our inordinate attachment to material things." View "is only a means to an end, a guide for goal-oriented action … [and] has only relative value, relative to the realization of the goal."

Comparison with the Market Economy

Arguably, economist determines what economics is based on his own value system and perception of reality (Alexandrin 1993). As illustrated above, Buddhist Economics is determined based on Buddhist world-view which are largely different from that of the market economy. Some of the ethical elements in Buddhist Economics are compatible with modern economics and could be reintroduced to modern economics for better social and environmental considerations. Alexandrin (1993) argues that by reintroducing Buddhist ethical elements into western economics, it provides all the economics and governments a broader theoretical discussion of ways to build their countries with skillful means depending on the local contexts. He proclaims that the essence of Buddhist Economics is the enlightened mind which empowers humans to see time and universe at present and beyond present. Buddhist Economics attempts to understand humans as they are—or could be:

> its premise is that economics is also education... . Buddhist Economics emphasizes a belief in the powers of people and their ability to change their thoughts and actions and, thus, their economics and their environment. (Alexandrin 1993)

Zsolnai (2007, 2011) further highlights that the key principles of Buddhist Economics are minimizing suffering of all sentient beings, including non-human beings, simplifying desires, non-violence, genuine care, and generosity. He believes that reducing desires beyond minimum material comfort can "bring substantial benefits for the person, for the community, and for nature" (2008). It requires our actions to be non-violent and hence requires us to not cause harm and suffering to ourselves or others (2007). Instead of taking an instrumental approach to parties in economic activities, Buddhist Economics emphasizes "interconnectedness," suggesting that we should genuinely care about the stakeholders involved in our economic decisions. Zsolnai (2007) and Schumacher (1984) argue that Buddhist Economics focuses on using available resources to meet the needs of local people in the most efficient ways. They argue that a local economy with adequate technology and self-reliance would minimize violence to other stakeholders as a result of an unlimited desire for growth. Comparing with the Market Economics which is considered as a "dismal science," Buddhist Economics offers a holistic enlightened approach which integrates sustainability, equity, and compassion, contributing to a high quality of high in a sustainable world (Brown 2017b) (Table 5.2).

Table 5.2 Comparing core elements of market economy and Buddhist Economics

	Market economy	*Buddhist Economics*
Participants	"Economic man" of Adam Smith	*Buddha*, *Bodhisatta* Monastics, lay practitioners
Principles of reasoning and motivation	Rationality Maximizing profits Minimizing expenses Optimizing economic results More is more Bigger is better Endless technological race	Middle way, threefold trainings, four Noble truths, Noble eightfold path, selflessness, dependent-arising Minimizing suffering, desires, violence, instrumental use Less is more Small is beautiful Adequate/appropriate technology
Variables	Utility, profits, expenses, consumption, work/employment, investment Margin rate of change, utility, productivity, efficiency Bias towards measurable quantity Price contains sufficient information to disengage moral responsibilities "Market" size and share	Moral discipline Mindfulness, perseverance, patience Wisdom Noble eightfold path (e.g. right livelihood) Compassion, generosity, non-violence, genuine care, no-harm, equity Price is not sufficient information for responsible decision-making Tangible things as well as intangible qualities and values
World-view	"Dismal science" Optimization based on one point in time and space Identities constructed based on economic activities Most subjects are reducible to exchangeable commodities Exchange across time and space through temporal choices and global trade Bias toward here and now ignoring interests of those under/not represented	Enlightened holistic approach Dependent-arising Selflessness Karmic causes and consequences over time Material and spiritual developments are all worthy Sustainability over time and space Local sufficiency and self-reliance Multiple universes
Behavioral forces	Greed/desire, fear, ignorance Self-interest Market-driven by the invisible hand Economic welfare as the ends Material well-being	Cessation of suffering, Compassion and wisdom Mind-driven by each individual's choices Spiritual advancement as the ends Overall well-being
Relationship	Competition, zero-sum game, win-lose Instrumental use—relationship as means	Collaboration, co-operation, win-win Relational—relationship as ends

Source: Author with reference to Alexandrin (1993), Zadek (1993, 1997), Alexandrin and Zech (1999), Zsolnai (2007, 2011), Brown (2017b)

Buddhist Economics as a Strategy and Way of Life

Zsolnai (2008) proposes that Buddhist Economics is "not a system but a strategy." It "does not aim to build an economic system" and should be applicable "in any economic setting at any time." In other words, Buddhist Economics as a strategy could be adopted in a range of economic models, including the market economy, with or without Buddhist background. The challenging is how Buddhist values should interact with the market economy, which has become the dominating and entrenched system. Similar cases have been observed in the interaction between religion and social development in the Theravada traditions. The religion-social idea in these traditions is an ongoing development by human actions. Any economic and social strategy must also "be structured according to the ideal if the social order is to embody it" (Reynolds and Clifford 1980).

Buddhist Economics should not be subject to the instrumental view of the markets. Zadek (1993) argues that it "[should] turn this equation on its head and insists rather that economic development must cohere with Buddhist values." The core objective of Buddhist Economics is based on practices in which overall well-being is enhanced, not jeopardized by material possessions. Economic welfare is instrumental in achieving spiritual advancement, not the other way around. Accommodating the modern market economy by picking and choosing selected concepts of Buddhism into Western economics might risk stripping Buddhist values of its context.

Zadek (1997) challenges Buddhists and scholars to approach Buddhist Economics differently by offering a way of practicing economy in a manner that is consistent with Buddhist principles and values, addressing some of the shortcomings of the market economy through a Buddhist path of both resistance and reconstruction:

> The question is not merely whether there is or is not a Buddhist Economics… . It is whether we can conceive of an economics that embodies the values that we espouse and try to live by. It is how we can best reflect personal practice and canonical ideals in the social domain, particularly with the sphere of economy.

Goulet (1980) also advises that intangible values must not be treated in a purely instrumental way. He argues that a non-instrumental treatment of values is in fact more humane and efficient because "indigenously-rooted values are the matrix whence people derive meaning in [their] lives, a sense of identity and cultural integrity, and the experience of continuity with their environment and their past even in the midst of change." These traditional values "harbour within them a latent dynamism which, when properly respected, can serve as the springboard for modes of development which are more humane than those drawn from outside paradigms" (Goulet 1980). Using the *Sarvodaya* movement as an example, any successful social and economic changes have to be consistent with the fundamental moral and spiritual goals. These economic changes are only a means to an end, which comprises many other aspects of developments (Ariyaratne 1982).

Chapter Summary

- Buddhist teachings never praised poverty or suffering. In fact, the ultimate goal of Buddhism is the cessation of suffering. However, its understanding of happiness and suffering and the means to pursuit happiness is very different from that in the world.
- Cessation of suffering in Buddhist teachings would require know and see the truth about the real nature of our "self" and our experience world.
- There is an inseparable causal correlation between morality and happiness. Morally good is "skillful" as evaluated by our mind which is "skillful", "pure", "well", and "in freedom", i.e. a mind that is "happy".
- To be happy we need to keep our mind under control with the cultivation of mindfulness and clear comprehension. We are responsible for our happiness as much as we are responsible for our moral actions.
- Buddhist Economics is "Buddhist" because it is consistent with the teachings of the *Buddha*: The Middle Way, the Noble Eightfold Path, the Four Noble Truths, the Threefold Training of moral discipline, mental concentration, and wisdom. In particular, wisdom is distinctive for Buddhist Economics in terms of the principle of selflessness, dependent arising, the right view, and so forth.
- Buddhist Economics are different from the Market Economics in many aspects. In particular, its essence is the enlightened mind and the endeavors to understand humans as they are. It is humanistic and genuinely care for the community and environment.
- It could contribute more to society and environment if it is being adopted as a strategy instead of a system, applicable to any economic setting at any time. It should not be subject to the instrumental view of the markets.

Study Questions

- How is the definition of suffering and happiness in Buddhism different from the market economy?
- How is the means of pursuing happiness in Buddhism different from that in the market?
- What is suffering according to Buddhist teachings?
- What is the relationship between morality and happiness in Buddhist philosophies?
- Does Buddhist Economics inhibit economic growth?
- What makes Buddhist Economics "Buddhist"?
- Is Buddhist Economics a "system" or a "strategy"?

Suggested Essay Topics

- Pursuit of happiness in the market and Buddhism
- Moral and happiness in Buddhist Economics
- Material and spiritual well-being
- Comparative analyses of Buddhist Economics and Market Economics
- Elements of Buddhist Economics
- Buddhist Economics as a strategy

Bibliography

Online Multimedia

Brown, Clair. 2017a. Buddhist Economics by Clair Brown. Last modified 3 February 2017. https://www.youtube.com/watch?v=88RX5A2iezs&feature=youtu.be

Required Reading

Alexandrin, Glen. 1993. Elements of Buddhist Economics. *International Journal of Social Economics* 20 (2): 3–11.

Karunadasa, Yakupitiyage. 2013. Pursuit of Happiness. In *Early Buddhist Teachings: The Middle Position in Theory and Practice*, 105–118. Hong Kong: Centre of Buddhist Studies, The University of Hong Kong. Reprint, Second 2015.

Zsolnai, László. 2008. Buddhist Economic Strategy. In *Frugality: Rebalancing Material and Spiritual Values in Economic Life*, ed. Luk Bouckaert, Hendrik Opdebeeck, and László Zsolnai, 279–304. Oxford: Peter Lang Publishing.

Further Reading

Alexandrin, Glen, and Charles Zech. 1999. Ancient Futures: Papal and Buddhist Economics. *International Journal of Social Economics* 26 (10/11): 1344–1353.

Ariyaratne, Ahangamage. 1982. *Collected Works Volume I*. Moratuwa: Sarvodaya Publication.

Bodhi, Bhikkhu. 2000. *The Connected Discourses of the Buddha, a Translation of the Saṃyutta Nikāya*. Somerville: Wisdom Publications.

———. 2012. *The Numerical Discourses of the Buddha: A Translation of the Anguttara Nikaya*. Translated by from Pali by Bhikkhu Bodhi. Somerville: Wisdom Publications.

———. 2013. Transcendental Dependent Arising: A Translation and Exposition of the Upanisa Sutta. In *Access to Insight* (BCBS Edition). Last modified 1 December 2013. http://www.accesstoinsight.org/lib/authors/bodhi/wheel277.html

Brown, Clair. 2017b. *Buddhist Economics*. New York: Bloomsbury Press.

CDB. SN 12.23. *Nidānasaṃyutta* (Connected Discourses on the Causation), *Proximate Cause*. In *CDB*, 553–556. Somerville: Wisdom Publications.

CDB. SN 56.11. *Saccasaṃyutta* (Connected Discourses on the Truths), *Dhammacakkappavattana Sutta* (Setting in Motion the Wheel of the Dhamma). In *CDB*, 1843–1847. Somerville: Wisdom Publications.

CDB. SN 56.35. *Saccasaṃyutta* (Connected Discourses on the Truths), A Hundred Spears. In *CDB*, 1860. Somerville: Wisdom Publications.

Gethin, Rupert. 1998. Four Truths: The Disease, the Cause, the Cure, the Medicine. In *The Foundations of Buddhism*, 59–79. Oxford/New York: Oxford University Press.

Goulet, Denis. 1980. Development Experts: The One-Eyed Giants. *World Development* 8 (7/8): 481–489.

Karunadasa, Yakupitiyage. 2015. *Early Buddhist Teachings: The Middle Position in Theory and Practice*. Hong Kong: Centre of Buddhist Studies, The University of Hong Kong.

MLDB. MN 18. Madhupiṇḍika Sutta: The Honeyball. In *MLDB*, 201–206. Somerville: Wisdom Publications.

MLDB. MN 2. Sabbasava Sutta: All the Taints. In *MLDB*, 91–97. Somerville: Wisdom Publications.

Ñanamoli, Bhikkhu, and Bhikkhu Bodhi. 1995. *The Middle Length Discourses of the Buddha: A Translation of the Majjhima Nikaya (Teachings of the Buddha)*. Somerville: Wisdom Publications.

NDB. AN 1.306. One Thing Sutta. In *NDB*, 117–118. Somerville: Wisdom Publications.

NDB. AN 1.308. One Thing Sutta. In *NDB*, 117–118. Somerville: Wisdom Publications.

NDB. AN 1.312. One Thing Sutta. In *NDB*, 117–118. Somerville: Wisdom Publications.

NDB. AN 1.314. One Thing Sutta. In *NDB*, 117–118. Somerville: Wisdom Publications.

Reynolds, Frank E., and Regina T. Clifford. 1980. Sangha, Society, and the Struggle for National Identity: Burma and Thailand. In *Transitions and Transformations in the History of Religions: Essays in Honor of Joseph M. Kitagawa*, ed. Frank E. Reynolds and Theodore M. Ludwig, 56–91. Leiden: E. J. Brill.

Schumacher, Ernst F. 1984. *Small Is Beautiful: Economics as if People Mattered*. London: Sphere Books Ltd. Original edition, 1973.

Sn 3.12. Dvayatanupassana Sutta: The Noble One's Happiness. Translated from the Pāli by John Ireland. In *Access to Insight* (BCBS Edition). Last modified 30 November 2013. http://www.accesstoinsight.org/tipitaka/kn/snp/snp.3.12.irel.html

Ud 6.4. Tittha Sutta: Sectarians (1). Translated from the Pāli by Thanissaro Bhikkhu. In *Access to Insight* (Legacy Edition). Last modified 3 September 2012. http://www.accesstoinsight.org/tipitaka/kn/ud/ud.6.04.than.html

Zadek, Simon. 1993. The Practice of Buddhist Economics? Another View. *American Journal of Economics and Sociology* 52 (4): 433–445.

———. 1997. Towards a Progressive Buddhist Economics. In *Entering the Realm of Reality: Towards Dharmmic Societies*, ed. Jonathan Watts, Alan Senauke, and Santikaro Bhikkhu, 241–277. Bangkok: INEB.

Zsolnai, László. 2007. Western Economics Versus Buddhist Economics. *Society and Economy* 29 (2): 145–153.

———. 2011. Buddhist Economics. In *Handbook of Spirituality and Business*, 88–94. London: Palgrave Macmillan.

CHAPTER 6

Buddhist Ethics and Moral Life

Buddhist Ethics and Moral Theory

Moral discipline (Pāli: *sīla*) in Buddhist teachings is not an imposition from above by a supreme deity, nor is it an invention on the part of the *Buddha* (Karunadasa 2015). It is inherent in life, a special case of the principle of cause and effect. The *Buddha* only discovers the path to purify vision and put an end to suffering; "It's for you to strive ardently. *Tathagatas* simply point out the way" (Dhp v.274-276). Karunadasa (2015) emphasizes that the *Buddha* is a moral authority—not in the sense that he has authoritative power to impose his "moral will," but in the sense that he has authoritative knowledge on the subject of morality. Buddhist ethics are not coercive, but persuasive; more descriptive than prescriptive. The Buddhist evaluation of what is morally good and bad is not relative in the sense that it does not change in relation to shifting social conventions, cultural norms, government-enforced laws, or political ideologies (see *Kālāma Sutta: To the Kālāmas* in Box 6.1). The *Buddha* does not endorse dogmatic adherence to views, even if they are right. It is because of the fact that a view, in Buddhism, is only a guide to action; if it is called the "right view", it is because it leads us properly to the right goal, which is a right vision (Pāli: *sammā dassana*) into the true nature of the world both within and outside us (Pāli: *yathābhūtañāṇa*).

Moral discipline is the foundation of the spiritual path in Buddhism with different levels of practice suiting different levels of commitment

E. C. H. Ng, *Introduction to Buddhist Economics*,
Studies in Buddhist Economics, Management, and Policy,
https://doi.org/10.1007/978-3-030-35114-4_6

(Harvey 2013). A moral life is not a burdensome duty or set of bare "oughts", but an uplifting source of happiness. However, the reason something is a good action is not simply because it brings pleasant karmic fruits to the person who does the action. Rather, such fruits come because an action is itself a blameless one which is "wholesome" (Pāli: *kusala*)– originated from and nurturing a morally healthy state of mind; and "skillful"– informed by wisdom (Cousins 1996; Harvey 2009). Similarly, if economic decisions and activities are the means to generate and enjoy wealth with the pursuit of happiness as the ultimate goal, the morality of our economic activities, as guided by wholesome and skillful state of mind, must be an integral part of our economic decisions (Fig. 6.1).

Buddhism considers morality in its "skillfulness" or "unskillfulness" based on psychology. A mind is "skillful" when it has "skillful" qualities such as generosity, compassionate love, and wisdom. Individuals experi-

Fig. 6.1 *Buddha* entering into *Parinibbāna*. Note: The reclining *Buddha* at Cave 16 of Bingling Temple Grottes, Gansu, PRC. (Source: Photo by author)

ence mental health (Pāli: *ārogya*), mental purity (Pāli: *anavajjatā*), and mental ability (Pāli: *cheka*), all of which result in mental happiness (Pāli: *sukha-vipāka*)—"It is a mind that is in harmony with actuality". In the opposite, a mind is "unskillful" (Pāli: *akusala*) when it has "unskillful" qualities such as greed, malice, and delusion, all of which result in a mind that is "defiled" (Pāli: *kiliṭṭha-citta*), "diseased" (Pāli: *ātura-citta*) and "in bondage" (Pāli: *avimutta-citta*). Such a mind cannot see things in their proper perspective. A defiled and diseased mind is in a state of disharmony with actuality (Karunadasa 2015).

Greed (Pāli: *lobha*), aversion/malice (Pāli: *dosa*), and delusion (Pāli: *moha*) are the three roots of all moral evils. Greed covers all degrees of ego-centric desire, longing, attachment, and grasping. Aversion includes all forms of ill-will, anger, animosity, irritation and annoyance, along with so-called righteous anger and moral indignation. Delusion is another expression for ignorance (Pāli: *avijjā*). It is the absence of clear comprehension and objectivity. In the opposite, absence of greed (Pāli: *alobha*), absence of aversion (Pāli: *adosa*), and absence of delusion (Pāli: *amoha*) are the three roots of moral good. It is with reference to these six roots comprising the unwholesome and the wholesome, that Buddhism makes its moral evaluation as morally unwholesome (Pāli: *akusala*) and morally wholesome (Pāli: *kusala*) (Karunadasa 2015).

Box 6.1 ***Kālāma Sutta: To the Kālāmas*** **(NDB. AN 3.65)**
In confronting deluded and conflicting views in the world, the *Buddha* also taught us not to subject ourselves to authority and popular opinion. We need to know for ourselves through deep reflection:

Now, *Kālāmas*, don't go by reports, by legends, by traditions, by scripture, by logical conjecture, by inference, by analogies, by agreement through pondering views, by probability, or by the thought, "This contemplative is our teacher." When you know for yourselves that, "These qualities are skillful; these qualities are blameless; these qualities are praised by the wise; these qualities, when adopted and carried out, lead to welfare and to happiness"—then you should enter and remain in them.

At the level of psychology, Karunadasa (2015) explains that moral wrongdoings exist and progress on three levels of: (1) latency (Pāli: *anusaya*), where our moral unskillful qualities are "asleep" below the surface-consciousness; and on (2) arising-all-around (Pāli: *pariyuṭṭhāna*) where what have been asleep are now fully awakened. Our mind's turbulence is expressed through negative emotions and excited feelings. With the necessary conditions, our latent thoughts will lead to the arising of emotions and feelings and will be further expressed externally (3) at the level of going beyond (Pāli: *vītikkama*) where what have awakened is expressed in the form of vocal and physical bodily actions. Morality is reflected through these mental-psychology-body activities. Buddhist ethics see the goodness or badness of an action as residing in a combination of: (a) the mental state, including will, that it springs from; (b) the (immediate predicable) effects on those to whom the action is directed; and (c) the virtues or vices that it expresses and helps to cultivate—so as to move towards the perfection of enlightenment (Harvey 2013).

Three Cardinal Principles of Buddhist Theory of Moral Life

There are three cardinal principles of the Buddhist Theory of Moral Life (Karunadasa 2015): *Kammavāda* (Pāli): advocacy of moral life and the recognition of moral consequences, the recognition that there is a causal correlation between what we do and what we reap; *Kiriyavāda* (Pāli): recognition of the need to do morally wholesome acts and to refrain from morally unwholesome acts; *Viriyavāda* (Pāli): recognition and provision for the role of human effort in the pursuit of moral life.

When the *Buddha* defines "*kamma*" as volition or willed action (Pāli: *cetanā*), he gives it a psychological meaning instead of simply "action".[1] Moral action is recognized through the intentionality of action, instead of the action itself. To account for the moral responsibility of any action, a purposeful intention is required, i.e. only willed action produces an effect that is eventually experienced by the actor. While *kamma* can manifest in three different ways: physically, vocally and mentally, it is not three but one, i.e., volition or intention. And it should be clearly distinguished from its result (Pāli: *vipāka*). More importantly, all moral cultivation, in Buddhism's view, should be based on knowledge and should be constantly

[1] "It is volition, bhikkhus, that I call kamma. For having willed, one acts by body, speech, or mind" (NDB. AN 6.63).

accompanied by awareness. As a result, the *naïve* innocence of a baby-boy based on sheer ignorance without awareness—nor is it consciously and deliberately cultivated—cannot be equated with moral perfection. The senses should be cultivated, not suppressed, to see things as they truly are (Pāli: *yathābhūta*). (Karunadasa 2015).

Accordingly, the *kamma*-based Buddhist ethics is an ethics of intention, an ethics of volition. There are two important Buddhist perspectives on *kamma*: the first is that Buddhism rejects *kammic* determinism or the view that all human experience is due to past *kamma*; the second is that we do not have to experience retribution for all previously committed *kamma* (Karunadasa 2015). From a Buddhist perspective, everybody is capable of reform and re-habitable.

Buddhist Economic Ethics

Buddhist teachings on non-attachment to worldly pleasure should be understood in the context of different levels of practices required for those interested in engaging in different levels of spiritual life. As Harvey (2000) argues, wealth provides laypeople opportunities for new expression and cultivation of non-attachment and temptation of self-indulgence. Nevertheless, non-attachment does not mean poverty or indebtedness. It is about how material things can be properly used without being entangled by them. Indeed, the *Buddha* teaches that poverty and indebtedness are a source of suffering in the world (NDB. AN 6.45) and that "hunger is the foremost illness..." (Dhp v.202-204).

The *Buddha* not only approves of people obtaining wealth, but also shows us the correct way of generating and using it through the middle way between the extremes of: (a) poverty, where people have insufficient means for a fulfilling life, and (b) a materialistic pursuit of wealth for their own sake (Harvey 2000).

Wealth: Definition, Generation and Use

Definition of Wealth

Buddhist teachings suggest that the proper generation and use of wealth must be based on moral considerations. Wealth, economic growth, and utilization of wealth are beyond the narrow notion of material wealth. The *Buddha* teaches there are five kinds of wealth: (1) faith, (2) virtuous behavior, (3) learning, (4) generosity, and (5) wisdom, (or two additional kinds of wealth: moral shame and moral dread (NDB. AN 7.5 and NDB. AN 7.6)) which the *Buddha* considers to be necessary to say that "one is not poor, that one's life is not lived in vain" (NDB. AN 5.47). When being asked about the astounding and amazing wealth of the *Migāra* of *Rohaṇa*, the *Buddha* says that gold and silver is a kind of wealth he does not deny. However, this kind of wealth can be taken away by fire, water, kings, thieves and displeasing heirs. The seven kinds of wealth he taught above cannot be taken away (NDB. AN 7.7).

The *Buddha* even makes a direct analogy between the suffering of poverty and indebtedness with the suffering of those lacking moral development. For laypersons, poverty, getting in debt, having to pay interest, being reproved, prosecuted and imprisoned as a result of failing to repay his indebtedness are indeed forms of suffering in the world. Similarly, the *Buddha* says:

> ... having no faith, no sense of moral shame, no moral dread, no energy, no wisdom in [cultivating] wholesome qualities, that a poor destitute, indigent person engages in misconduct by body, speech, and mind. This, I say, is his getting into debt. (NDB. AN 6.45)

Those who engaged in misconduct by body, speech and mind "heaps up a mass of evil kamma" (NDB. AN 6.45) and will suffer from bondage in the future life in certain animal realms or hell. The wise person who cultivates moral qualities and wisdom is free and happy in his present and future lives:

> With the destruction of the fetters of existence, for the stable one, rightly liberated, the knowledge occurs: "My liberation is unshakable." This is the supreme knowledge; this is unsurpassed happiness. Sorrowless, dust-free, and secure, this is the highest freedom from debt. (NDB. AN 6.45)

Generation of Wealth

The *Buddha* also teaches that "whatever means by which a clansman earns his living—whether by farming, trade, raising cattle, archery, government service, or some other craft" (NDB. AN 8.54), he is accomplished in initiative when he is skillful and diligent; possesses sound judgment about it in order to carry out and arrange it properly. This accomplishment is one of the four things leading to the welfare and happiness in this present life. The *Buddha* expects a layperson to acquire wealth worthy of praise and enjoyment by "energetic striving, strength of his arms, sweat of his brow, righteous wealth righteously gained" (NDB. AN 4.61). According to the *Buddha*, wealth accumulation through lies without seeing moral implications, (e.g. with tricks, fraud and lies) is to be "one-eyed". Only those who can acquire wealth through their efforts righteously, knowing wholesomeness from unwholesomeness, are said to be of two eyes (NDB. AN 3.29).

Buddhism puts a strong emphasis on right livelihood or right means to make a living. It believes that our physical and mental well-being is tied to the way we think and act every day. The *Buddha* recommends that all lay people observe a code of ethics (LDB. DN 31), including the precepts of not taking life, not taking what is not given, not lying, and not committing adultery. We are encouraged to engage in professions that facilitate positive character building while discouraging otherwise. Five specific trades, including trading in weapons (being an arms salesman), living beings (keeping animals for slaughter), meat (being a slaughterer, meat salesman, hunter or fisherman), intoxicants, and poisons, are also wrong livelihoods (NDB. AN 5.177).

Success in ethical livelihoods has been denoted in early Buddhist texts as a boon, and see a person's moral and spiritual qualities contributive to success, rather than in any way hindering it (Harvey 2000). These success-enhancing qualities include: (1) the four accomplishments in faith, virtuous behavior, generosity, and wisdom (NDB. AN 4.61); (2) five advantages in careful attention leading to good wealth, good reputation, confidence and assurance wherever one goes, dies unconfused, arises in a heavenly world after death (MLDB. MN 16); (3) vigilance (Pāli: *appamāda*) (SN 3.1) (4) turning of four wheels (dwelling in a suitable locality, relying on good persons, right resolution, and merits done in the past), which lead to greatness and abundance of wealth (NDB. AN 4.31).

On choosing a specific type of employment, the *Buddha* does not agree that humans should be born into certain employment or social classes. He believes "birth makes no distinctive mark . . . Distinction among human beings is purely verbal designation" (MLDB. MN 98), so the division of humans into different kinds of work or class is groundless. It is really by people's actions, not designation or birth, that makes the difference. In this sense, the *Buddha* is truly meritocratic, allowing for mobility across different functions of man depending on their capabilities, merits and what they can do.

Use of Wealth

According to Buddhism, wealth is only of benefit if being put to use; however much one holds onto it, one will be parted from it at death (Harvey 2000). Paradoxically, the only way to benefit from one's wealth after death is by generously giving it away before one dies: for "what's given is well salvaged," because of the karmic fruits this brings (SN 1.41).

The *Buddha* explains that there are four kinds of happiness (NDB. AN 4.62) achievable for a layperson through the proper use of wealth: (1) ownership, (2) enjoyment, (3) freedom from debt, and (4) blamelessness. The *Buddha* suggests that when a layperson could appreciate the happiness of freedom from debt, he would recall the happiness of ownership. While experiencing the happiness of enjoyment, a layperson will begin to see things clearly with wisdom. The happiness of blamelessness is the happiness and joy arising from blameless bodily, verbal and mental action. Accordingly, material happiness facilitates and provides the proper conditions for spiritual development. Faith, virtuous behavior, generosity, and wisdom are four things that can lead to a layperson's welfare and happiness in future lives (NDB. AN 8.54). Together with the four accomplishments: (1) initiative in earning a living, (2) protection, (3) good friendship, and (4) balanced living, i.e. neither too extravagant nor too frugal and making sure his income exceeds expenditure, there are eight accomplishments recommended by the *Buddha* (NDB. AN 8.75 and NDB. AN 8.76).

Laypeople are advised to divide their wealth into four portions, with one portion for day-to-day recurring expenses, two portions for investment in productive enterprises, and the remaining one in savings for use in hard times (LDB. DN 31). The *Buddha* conveys that wealth can serve as a buffer against uncertainties in weather, robbers, and enemies and be used to make "offerings to kin, guests, the deceased, and kings; and finally . . to recluses and monks" (Pryor 1990). Wealth can function as the ration to support spiritual development. When someone is in a state of physical suffering, his mind is not calm and not open to reason (Pryor 1990). In another *sutta* (NDB. AN 4.61), the *Buddha* offers four worthy causes for deploying wealth: (1) for the happiness of oneself and his family, workers, servants, friends and colleagues, and so forth; (2) provisions for losses that might arise on account of fire and floods, kings and bandits and unloved heirs; (3) five oblations of relatives, guests, ancestors, the king, and the deities; and (4) offering of alms to those ascetics and Brahmins in good practice.

The *Buddha* further elaborates that wealth has four sources of accretion: (1) avoid womanizing, (2) avoid drunkenness, (3) avoid gambling, and (4) cultivate good friendship, companionship, and comradeship. Failing to do these will ensure the dissipation of wealth (NDB. AN 8.54). Harvey (2000) also refers to the six ways of dissipating one's wealth discussed in the *Sigālovāda Sutta* (LDB. DN 16): addiction to strong drink and sloth-producing drugs … haunting the street at unfitting times, attending fairs, being addicted to gambling, keeping bad company, and habitual idleness.

The *Buddha* advocates a balanced way of life (Pāli: *samajivitata*) which enables individuals to enjoy the happiness of economic stability (Pāli: *atthisukha*) with the happiness of debtlessness (Pāli: *ananasukha*). If we are pursuing our basic needs, we can keep it simple. The *Buddha*, therefore, teaches how individual desires, if unchecked by contentment, can lead one to lose all sense of priority and become confused and muddled when dealing with scarcity and choice. His injunction to all is to enjoy maximum happiness with minimum possessions. Happiness dependent on the pursuit and attachment of outside impermanent consumption is in fact a key source of *duhhka* or suffering in Buddhism. Puntasen (2007) explains that happiness in Buddhism (Pāli: *sukha*) is "more associated with mental development than with any form of acquisition … *sukha* … at the highest level, known as *vimuttisukha*, or *sukha* gained from freedom from all defilements does not require anything more than necessities to maintain life." In Buddhist teachings, poverty can be a state of mind if we never think we have enough (Karunadasa 2015).

Chapter Summary

- Buddhist moral order is not an imposition from above by a supreme deity, nor is it an invention on the part of the *Buddha*. It is inherent in life, a special case of the principle of cause and effect.
- The *Buddha* only discovers it, "you yourselves ought to do what ought to be done."
- A moral life is not a burdensome duty or set of bare "oughts," but an uplifting source of happiness.
- There is an inseparable causal correlation between morality and happiness. Morally good leads to happiness, what is morally bad leads to unhappiness.

- Something is a good action is not simply because it brings pleasant karmic fruits to the person who does the action. Such fruits come because an action is itself a blameless, one which is "wholesome" (Pāli: *kusala*)—coming from a morally healthy state of mind, and nurturing this—and "*skillful*"—informed by wisdom
- "Skillfulness" or "unskillfulness" is based on psychology.
- Three cardinal principles of Buddhist theory of moral life: *Kammavāda, Kiriyavāda, Viriyavāda* (Pāli).
- Definition of wealth: five kinds of wealth: (1) faith, (2) virtuous behavior, (3) learning, (4) generosity, and (5) wisdom, (and two additional kinds of wealth (6) moral shame and (7) moral dread).
- Poverty and indebtedness in Buddhist teachings are described with reference to morality. Moral developments lead to one's life is not lived in vain.
- *Buddha* says that gold and silver is a kind of wealth he does not deny. However, this kind of wealth can be taken away by fire, water, kings, thieves and displeasing heirs.
- Wealth should be generated through right livelihood: "he is accomplished in initiative when he is skillful and diligent; possesses sound judgment about it in order to carry out and arrange it proper."
- Success in ethical livelihoods has been denoted in early Buddhist texts as a boon, and see a person's moral and spiritual qualities contributive to success, rather than in any way hindering it. It is really by people's actions, not designation or birth, that makes the difference.
- Four kinds of happiness from good use of wealth: (1) ownership, (2) enjoyment, (3) freedom from debt, and (4) blamelessness; The four accomplishments in life are: (1) faith, (2) virtuous behavior, (3) generosity, and (4) wisdom. Additional four accomplishments are: (1) initiative in earning a living, (2) protection, (3) good friendship, and (4) balanced living.
- Divide wealth into four portions, with one portion for day-to-day recurring expenses, two portions for investment in productive enterprises, and the remaining one in savings for use in hard times.
- The *Buddha* advocates a balanced way of life (Pāli: *samajivitata*).

Study Questions

- Is ethical livelihood practical? Does it hinder success instead of contributing to it?
- Is Buddhist moral theory also a dogmatic adherence to views?
- How is Buddhist moral theory based on psychology?
- Is *kamma* pre-deterministic?
- How is Buddhist definition of wealth different from that of the market economy?
- Is wealth material or spiritual?
- What is right livelihood?

Suggested Essay Topics

- Buddhist moral theory of life and happiness
- *Kamma*: Three cardinal principles of Buddhist theory of moral life
- Buddhist moral theory and its perspectives on human mind
- Buddhist Economic ethics
- Relationship between material and spiritual pursuit of wealth
- Right livelihood and economic life inspired by Buddhist ethics

Bibliography

Required Reading

Harvey, Peter. 2000. Economic Ethics. In *An Introduction to Buddhist Ethics: Foundations, Values and Issues*, 187–197. Cambridge: Cambridge University Press. Reprint, Seventh.

———. 2013. Buddhist Practices: Ethics. In *An Introduction to Buddhism: Teachings, History and Practices*, 2nd ed., 264–266. New York: Cambridge University Press. Original edition, 1990.

Further Reading

Bodhi, Bhikkhu. 2012. *The Numerical Discourses of the Buddha: A Translation of the Aṅguttara Nikāya*. Translated by from the Pāli by Bhikkhu Bodhi. Somerville: Wisdom Publications.

Cousins, Lance. 1996. Good or Skilful? *Kusala* in Canon and Commentary. *Journal of Buddhist Ethics, 3*, 136–64: http://blogs.dickinson.edu/buddhistethics/files/2010/04/cousins12.pdf

Dhp. v.202-204. Sukhavagga: Happy. (Dhp XV). Translated from Pāli by Thanissaro Bhikkhu. *Access to Insight*. Last modified 30 November 2013. http://www.accesstoinsight.org/tipitaka/kn/dhp/dhp.15.than.html

Dhp. v.274-276. Maggavagga: The Path (Dhp XX). Translated from the Pāli by Thanissaro Bhikkhu. *Access to Insight* (BCBS Edition). Last modified 30 November 2013. http://www.accesstoinsight.org/tipitaka/kn/dhp/dhp.20.than.html

Harvey, Peter. 2009. "The Approach to Knowledge and Truth in the Theravāda Record of the Discourses of the Buddha", "Theravāda Philosophy of Mind and the Person", "Theravāda Texts on Ethics". In *Buddhist Philosophy: Essential Readings*, ed. William Edelglass and Jay Garfield, 175–85, 265–74–175–85, 375–87. Oxford: Oxford University Press.

Karunadasa, Yakupitiyage. 2015. Theory of Moral Life. In *Teachings: The Middle Position in Theory and Practice*, ed. Early Buddhist, 79–94. Hong Kong: Centre of Buddhist Studies, The University of Hong Kong.

LDB. DN 16. Mahāparinibbāna Sutta: The Great Passing. In *LDB*, 231–277. Somerville: Wisdom Publications.

LDB. DN 31. Sigālaka Sutta: To Sigālaka Advice to Lay People. In *LDB*, 461–470. Somerville: Wisdom Publications.

MLDB. MN 98. Vāseṭṭha Sutta. In *MLDB*, 798–807. Somerville: Wisdom Publications.

Ñanamoli, Bhikkhu, and Bhikkhu Bodhi. 1995. *The Middle Length Discourses of the Buddha: A translation of the Majjhima Nikaya (Teachings of the Buddha)*. Somerville: Wisdom Publications.

NDB. AN 3.29. Blind. In *NDB*, 224–225. Somerville: Wisdom Publications.

NDB. AN 3.65. Kesaputtiya. In *NDB*, 279–283. Somerville: Wisdom Publications.

NDB. AN 4.31. The Wheel. In *NDB*, 419. Somerville: Wisdom Publications.

NDB. AN 4.61. Worthy Deeds. In *NDB*, 449–452. Somerville: Wisdom Publications.

NDB. AN 4.62. Freedom from Debt. In *NDB*, 452–453. Somerville: Wisdom Publications.

NDB. AN 5.177. Trades. In *NDB*, 790. Somerville: Wisdom Publications.

NDB. AN 5.47. Wealth. In *NDB*, 672–674. Somerville: Wisdom Publications.

NDB. AN 6.45. Debt. In *NDB*, 914–917. Somerville: Wisdom Publications.

NDB. AN 6.63. Penetrative. In *NDB*, 963. Somerville: Wisdom Publications.

NDB. AN 7.5. Wealth in Brief. In *NDB*, 1000. Somerville: Wisdom Publications.

NDB. AN 7.6. Wealth in Detail. In *NDB*, 1000–1001. Somerville: Wisdom Publications.

NDB. AN 7.7. Ugga. In *NDB*, 1001–1002. Somerville: Wisdom Publications.

NDB. AN 8.54. Dīghajānu. In *NDB*, 1194–1197. Somerville: Wisdom Publications.

Pryor, Frederic L. 1990. A Buddhist Economic System. In Principle: Non-Attachment to Worldly Things Is Dominant But the Way of the Law Is Held Profitable. *American Journal of Economics and Sociology* 49 (3): 339–349.

Puntasen, Apichai. 2007. *Why Buddhist Economics Is Needed as a New Paradigm for a Better Understanding of Happiness (Wellness)*. Bangkok: International Conference on Happiness and Public Policy.

SN 1.41. Aditta Sutta (The House) on Fire. Translated from Pāli by Thanissaro Bhikkhu. *Access to Insight (BCBS Edition)*. Last modified 30 November 2013. http://www.accesstoinsight.org/tipitaka/sn/sn01/sn01.041.than.html

SN 3.1. Dahara Sutta: Young. Translated from Pāli by Thanissaro Bhikkhu. *Access to Insight (BCBS Edition)*. Last modified 30 November 2013. https://www.accesstoinsight.org/tipitaka/sn/sn03/sn03.001.than.html

Walshe, Maurice. 1986. *The Long Discourses of the Buddha: A Translation of the Dīgha Nikāya*. Translated by from the Pāli by Maurice Walshe. Somerville: Wisdom Publications.

CHAPTER 7

Buddhist Wisdom and Defining Principles

Wisdom: Knowledge of Phenomena as They Really Are

Wisdom (Pāli: *paññā*) in Buddhism is the ability to understand everything in this world, both internal and external of ourselves, truly, as it is. It comprises accurate and practical insights into how things originate and cease to exist, including our mental and bodily activities. It "is not the knowledge of some kind of transcendental reality. … Rather, it is the final awakening to the actual phenomenal existence" (Karunadasa 2015b). While we experience and understand this world through our sensory faculties, Buddhist teachings suggest that there are also different means of knowledge (e.g. extra-sensory perception) and different level of knowledge (Karunadasa 2015a). Wisdom is a proper understanding of the phenomenal existence as impermanence (Pāli: *anicca*), suffering (Pāli: *dukkha*), and selflessness (Pāli: *anatta*). In the opposite, ignorance is the failure to realize the dependent arising of the internal and external world. It is the improper understanding of the phenomenal existence as permanence, blissful, and self.

Wisdom is an important component of the Threefold Training in the spiritual path leading to enlightenment. It depends on both conceptual and intellectual understanding with meditative insight, including but not limited to various teachings such as the Four Noble Truths, moral theory of cause and consequence, and so forth (Cantwell 2010). In the Noble Eightfold Path, right view, on the one hand, is the understanding of the Four Noble

E. C. H. Ng, *Introduction to Buddhist Economics*,
Studies in Buddhist Economics, Management, and Policy,
https://doi.org/10.1007/978-3-030-35114-4_7

Truths and conditioned existence in terms of suffering, impermanence and selflessness, and the path to liberation. Right effort, on the other hand, acts together with the right view and promises to renounce worldly goals to bring benefit rather than harm to oneself and others (Cantwell 2010).

The doctrine of dependent arising and selflessness is a unique contribution of Buddhist teachings. In the context of Buddhist Economics, wisdom means a deeper understanding of: (1) the behavior of each decision-maker; (2) interaction between each building block of the economic decision process; and (3) the decisions and actions required to achieve the objectives of economic activities. Through the doctrine of dependent arising, we understand the inevitable arising as well as the cessation of growth, human behavior and other interdependent phenomena in the market. Through the doctrine of selflessness, we understand the arising of identity within an organization and how individual interacts and interrelated to another including rest of the community and ecosystem.

Another important Buddhist wisdom for decision-making process in the market and society is the notion of "view": (1) wrong views and (2) attachment to views. To enable us to perceive and understand the risks and uncertainties we encounter daily, we need to think with an open mind and an open heart, and appreciate all perspectives and scenarios. From a Buddhist perspective, it is nearly impossible, if not wrong, to aim at a perfect model to predict and manage risks and uncertainties. The complex web of relationship among different facts, events and economic actions and how they interact altogether contribute to the uncertainties observed. To ensure that our views are beneficial to others, the environment, and ourselves, we need to embrace a decision-making framework based on sustainable values. Instead of a rigid, all-knowing, or overconfident mindset, if we start with a mind full of possibility, curiosity, and humility—Zen's "Don't Know Mind"—we could alleviate clashes of ideas within ourselves (the past, present, or future), or conflicts between one another. These conflicts usually turn into battles of ego and identity, without contributing to the genuine progress of humanity.

Dependent Arising: Nothing Arises Alone Independent of Other Conditions

To explain the origination of things in this world, the *Buddha* rejects any dualistic views advocated by other schools of thought. He proclaims the doctrine of dependent arising (Pāli: *paṭiccasamuppāda*):

> when this exists, that comes to be; with the arising of this, that arises ... when this does not exist, that does not come to be; with the cessation of this, that ceases. (MLDB. MN 39)

According to Karunadasa (2001), it is defined "to mean the arising of phenomena in dependence on other phenomena, with no unchanging substance behind the phenomena." This formula shows that whatever arises is arising in dependence on conditions; whatever ceases is ceasing because of those conditions that made it arise. Although the formula states just one condition for each subsequent link, this should not be taken as a suggestion that a single "cause" is sufficient for the arising of each further link (Gethin 1998). Each condition is stated as a representative and significant cause. It describes a process, and we usually conceive of processes, by definition, as taking place over a period of time. Yet for the *Abhidhamma* (Pāli), such a process occurs quite literally in one moment: the twelve factors arise simultaneously. The "cause" in Buddhism is "neither a substantial entity, nor an active agent." It does not have its "own-sway/own-power" (Pāli: *vasavattitā*) to produce the effect (Karunadasa 2015a).

In a cognitive process, for example, all mental phenomena, such as attention and perception, take place naturally according to the principles of psychological order (Pāli: *cittaniyāma*). Each stage in the continuum is being conditioned by the immediately preceding one, with no substance passing from one stage to another. To be precise, the doctrine of dependent arising illustrates that "nothing arising from nothing, nothing arises from a single condition, nothing arises as a single conditioned factor. It is always the case that from a multiplicity of conditions arise a multiplicity of conditioned factors". Strictly speaking, "dependent" means "co-dependent," and "arising" means "co-arising" (Karunadasa 2015a). Buddhism concentrates not on the origin or end of the order, but on the order itself.

According to Karunadasa (2015a), dependent arising is presented as "the middle doctrine," because it steers clear of the mutual conflict between (1) spiritual eternalism and materialist annihilationism, (2) "all exists" (Pāli: *sabbaṃatthi*) and "all does not exist" (Pāli: *sabbaṃnatthi*), (3) "all are a unity" (Pāli: *sabbaṃekattaṃ*) and "all are a plurality" (Pāli: *sabbaṃputhuttaṃ*), (4) self-causation (Pāli: *sayaṃ-kata*) and external causation (Pāli: *paraṃ-kata*), (5) strict determinism and strict indeterminism, (6) the absolute beginning of the universe (Pāli: *pubbanta-kappika*) and the ultimate direction it is heading for (Pāli: *aparanta-kappika*).

Taking this understanding of selflessness and depending arising into the dharmas (components which combine to form people and things), *Mahāyāna* (Skt.) Buddhism integrated early Buddhist understanding of wisdom into a broader understanding which introduced the idea of a transcendent wisdom. The main thrust of mainstream Buddhist doctrine, as we have seen, is that such combinations of dharmas are empty of any fixed self (Cantwell 2010). As we will further explore, it is this deep wisdom of selflessness and emptiness that allows for genuine care, collaboration, and compassion. With the appreciation of dependent arising, we can truly see the interdependent nature of each individual with our society, environment, and rest of the ecosystem.

Buddhaghosa gives us the following vivid image of dependent arising (Gethin 1998): A blind man (ignorance) stumbles (formations) and falls (consciousness); as a result of the fall, a swelling develops (mentality-materiality) and on that swelling, there forms an abscess which weeps (six senses); this abscess gets continually knocked and bruised (contact) causing terrible pain (feeling) which the man longs to remove (craving); in consequence, he seizes on (grasping) and applies (becoming) to the swelling various remedies that he thinks will relieve the pain; but instead of relieving the pain, their effect is simply to change the condition of the swelling for the worse (birth) and finally the whole swelling bursts (old age and death).

"Mentality" in the compound mentality-materiality denotes the five aggregates. It is important to note that at every stage of the process, all the five aggregates of grasping are present. When sensory contact arises, it cannot arise as a single factor. It arises together with all the five aggregates of grasping, excluding sensory contact. As Karunadasa (2015a) expounds, if only sensory contact is mentioned, this is done in order to relate the most important conditioned factor among a collection of other conditioned factors. The situation is true for feeling as well.

From the Buddhist perspective, all compounded phenomena are subject to change—impermanence; there is no permanent "self" who experiences an ever-lasting external world. We are hardly the "masters" of our "selves," let alone masters of the external world. This is because even our sense of identity is dependently arising—birth, decay, aging, and death are not only natural but inevitable. Our identity on its own, or in relation to our work or family, is subject to all the constituent factors, which are also subject to arising and cessation. Buddhist teachings illustrate a completely different perspective of selflessness. If there is no permanent "self" under our control, how can we talk about meaningful ownership or sustainable happiness that builds upon the unsustainable nature of this world?

Failing to understand change as part of life fixates us to the status quo of like or dislike. We fail to tolerate the fact that not only the "object" changes, the subject ("we"), who experiences, are also constantly changing. Rarely will someone despise a new workplace or personal relationship when it begins, yet our attitudes toward the workplace or other people can easily change over time because people and situations evolve, and our own perspectives and perceptions also change. Even more alarmingly, we can be deceived by the calm before the storm. In reality, situations are often multifaceted, complex, and unstable.

Box 7.1 Twelve-Factored Formula of Dependent Arising (CDB. SN 12.1)
"And what, Bhikkus, is dependent origination?

With ignorance (Pāli: *avijā*) as condition, volitional formations (Pāli: *sankhāra*) [come to be];
with volitional formations as condition, consciousness (Pāli: *viññana*);
with consciousness as condition, name-and-form (Pāli: *nāmarūpa*);
with name-and-form as condition, six sense bases (Pāli: *saḷāyatana*);
with six sense bases as condition, contact (Pāli: *phassa*);
with contact as condition, feeling (Pāli: *vedanā*);
with feeling as condition, craving (Pāli: *taṇhā*),
with craving as condition, clinging (Pāli: *upādāna*);
with clinging as condition, existence (Pāli: *bhava*);
with existence as condition, birth (Pāli: *jāti*);
with birth as condition, aging-and-death, sorrow, lamentation, pain, displeasure, and despair (Pāli: *jarāmaraṇaṃsokaparidevadukkhad-omanassupāyāsa*) come to be. Such is the origin of this whole mass suffering. This, Bhikkhus, is called dependent origination."

Five Aggregates, Six Senses and the Notion of Self: Knowledge of Our "Self"

By applying the doctrine of dependent arising into the analysis and synthesis of our self-entity and reality, we could understand that the nature of reality is in fact centered on impermanence (Pāli: *anicca*), while the nature of self is in fact selflessness (Pāli: *anatta*). The *Buddha* argues that there is "no independent self-entity, mental or material, which is impervious to change" (Karunadasa 2001). Humans perceive the external world and our material self through the five senses of sight, hearing, smell, taste, and touch. Together with mental activities, either in response to the physical stimuli or not, our physical and mental events can be attributed to the five "aggregates" or "groups" (Pali: *khandha*-s). They are usually described as the five aggregates of grasping because they are not static entities but five constantly changing aspects of individual existence, which always interact with the external world. It is therefore "not correct to say that they exist, nor is it correct to say that they do not exist" (Karunadasa 2015a).

These five aggregates are: (1) form aggregate (Pāli: *rūpa*) as well as mental aggregates including (2) sensation/feelings (Pāli: *vedanā*), (3) perceptions/recognition (Pāli: *saññā*), (4) mental volitional "forces" or "formations/fabrication" (Pāli: *saṅkhāra*) and (5) self-consciousness (Pāli: *viññāna*). From the clinging of our perceptions, we further fabricate a self-identity in terms of the five aggregates because our "perceptions" should only be "justified" if there is a continuous existence "I" with the ability to cling (MLDB. MN 109) (Fig. 7.1).

These physical and mental activities lead us to wonder, "who" or "what" is the subject of all these experiences. "Who" is entitled or holds ownership over these experiences? As Gethin (1998) argues, Buddhist teachings explain that linguistic usage, certain emotional and psychological circumstances predispose us to an understanding of personal identity and selfhood in terms of an 'I' that independently exists and experiences. In this process, we assume—perhaps unconsciously—that an "I" / "me" may exist and remain constant even though my experience may come and go. This perspective is in fact one of the four kinds of problematic and erroneous clinging: (1) clinging to sense pleasure (Pāli: *kāma-upādāna*), (2) clinging to speculative views on the nature of the self and the world (Pāli: *diṭṭhi-upādāna*), (3) clinging to rites and observances as a means to salvation (Pāli: *sīlabbata-upādāna*), and (4) clinging to a doctrine of self (Pāli: *attavāda-upādāna*) (Karunadasa 2015a).

On one hand, this notion of self as a permanent, truly existent identity can be born of delusion (Pāli: *moha*) or ignorance (Pāli: *avijjā*)—the failure to perceive the world as it actually is. On the other hand, it can also originate from our craving (Pāli: *taṇha*) and attachment (Pāli: *upādāna*)—the sense of 'self' springs not only from delusion, but from the desire to identify (Gethin 1998). This construction of self is not only at the conscious and intellectual level, but also at a deep psychological and emotional level. Karunadasa (2015a) explains that according to Buddhism, every cognitive

Fig. 7.1 International Buddhist flag. Note: The international Buddhist flag with bands in blue, yellow, red, white, and orange. (Source: Photo by author)

act consists of a series of cognitive events. In these events, the latent tendency for the ego-consciousness awakens, solidifies and eventually crystallizes at the final stage called conceptual proliferations (Pāli: *papañca*). Once the ego-consciousness has arisen, it cannot exist in a vacuum: it needs an ontological support. Whenever an unenlightened person perceives through the sensory faculties, he also automatically conceives—through an "individual" who actively conceives and owns the experience. Self-identity is the expression of mental fabrication from clinging to the bases of our perceptions and the notion of self (MLDB. MN 102). This clinging process is expressed in three ways: "This is mine (Pāli: *etaṃ mama*), this is I am (Pāli: *esohamasmi*), and this is my self (Pāli: *eso me attā*).

The first is due to craving (Pāli: *taṇhā*); the second to conceit (Pāli: *māna*); and the third is due to mistaken belief in a self-entity (Pāli: *diṭṭhi*)." Sufferings and conflicts arise as a result of "identifying ourselves with what is impermanent (Pāli: *anicca*), with what does not come under our full control (*anatta*)" (Karunadasa 2015a). Together with greed, hatred, and ignorance we misconceive that some parts of the internal and external world belong to us, are controlled by us, or are identified with us. Craving, conceit, and view are thus three different aspects of the ego-consciousness. This is the wrong view of selflessness as self.

Selflessness: Who Is Really There?

Karunadasa (2015a) believes the notion of self has many forms: the first version is based on the duality between the self and the body; and the second version is based on the identity of self and the body. The Buddhist idea of non-self is based on the denial of both versions. This clinging to self can also be defined as "the aggregation (Pāli: *saṅgaha*) collocation (Pāli: *sannipāta*), and coming-together (Pāli: *samavāya*) of the five aggregates of clinging". Using materiality as an example, we misunderstand it as our "self" by assuming that: (1) materiality is the same as the self, (2) the self possesses materiality, (3) materiality is within the self, or (4) the self is in materiality.

Buddhist teachings do not deny the fact that we are the sum of the five aggregates combined. However, these five aggregates and the combination are constantly in a state of flux under the doctrine of dependent arising. What is in a state of constant flux is impermanent, not under one's full control and mastery, and hence a source of suffering and "non-self" (Karunadasa 2015a). What Buddhism denies is not the concept of the person (Pāli: *puggala*), but a self-subsisting entity within the person.

Individual existence is not self-subsisting. It requires four kinds of food to support its operations through the process of nutriment or alimentation (Karunadasa 2015a). In addition to physical food and drink we eat and drink to keep our physical body alive—"morsel-made-food" (Pāli: *kabalīkāra-āhāra*)—three other kinds of food are required: (1) sensory contact (*phassa*), (2) mental volition (Pāli: *manosañcetanā*), and (3) consciousness (Pāli: *viññaṇa*). Amongst these, mental volition is the conative or motivating aspect. It is the most dynamic, indeed, the will to live. The fourth kind of food, which is consciousness, has to be understood in the context of the process of *saṃsāra* (Pāli), the cycle of births and deaths (Karunadasa 2015a). Since individual existence is neither self-subsisting nor permanent, it requires nutriments and proper conditions for support. Our mind and body are out of our control, subject to change and sickness, and hence "painful" and "suffering" (Pāli: *duhkha*) if we become attached. (Gethin 1998). Buddhist teaching on non-self is "intended as a remedy for the belief in self-entity" (Karunadasa 2015a).

To overcome this erroneous attachment to self, Buddhist teachings approach it from the analysis of the individual experience. Firstly, if we identify our "self" with changing experiences, there should be no "self" because it continuously changes as our experiences change. If "self" is supposed to remain constant behind changing experiences, then self cannot be the same as our experiences. Secondly, if 'I' exist apart from our experiences, how can we think of oneself as existing? Thirdly, if self is different from our experiences, yet not without experiences a self that experiences or has the attribute of experience—then there must be scenarios where such a self is still distinguishable from experiences. Yet there is no basis upon which to make such a distinction since it remains that apart from particular experiences, it is not possible to think of oneself as existing. Following the analyses above, Buddhist teachings propose that an individual is a complex flow of physical and mental phenomena, but without these phenomena, we just cannot identify a constant self as our identity.

To account for our experienced "facts" of personal continuity or stability, the *Buddha* teaches that this identity does not reside in some enduring substantial self-entity in our lifespan but in clusters of physical and mental events (the eighteen "elements" (Pāli: *dhātu*): six senses, six of sense object, and six classes of consciousness) which are linked causally (Gethin 1998). This apparent stability of events is only relative to the conditions sustaining it. Eventually this stability will collapse when the conditions supporting it cease to exist. However, as soon as one particular configuration breaks down, another configuration may raise when other conditions arise. Just as this causal connectedness is the basis of continuity within our present lifespan, this causal connectedness continues despite the death of a "person" and explains the continuity between lives.

This understanding of causal connectedness shows that the Buddhist doctrine of selflessness is not a nihilism—negation of a "person" or moral responsibilities. References to "me" and "I" are perfectly normal in Buddhist discourse, but it is important to distinguish between the conventional (Pāli: *sammuti*) and ultimate (Pāli: *paramattha*) truth (Gethin 1998). References are believed to be dissimilar to any of the components (Pāli: *khanda*-s) of the empiric individuality taken selectively or collectively, but transcends them on both levels (Karunadasa 2015a).

Notwithstanding the stability and continuity in us that is built upon causality, it is not permanent. While impermanence tends to carry negative connotations, it makes transformation and the ultimate transformation possible. In Buddhist teachings, the characteristic of non-self (*anatta*) is often presented with impermanence and suffering: what is impermanent is suffering (*yad aniccaṃ taṃ dukkhaṃ*); what is suffering is non-self (Pāli: *yaṃ dukkhaṃ tad anattā*) (Karunadasa 2015a). The idea of non-self should not be understood in isolation from dependent arising. Once we understand the doctrine of dependent arising and selflessness, we should appreciate how individuals are inseparable from society and the rest of the ecosystem. Each of us shares the same fortune and misfortune of the rest of society and ecosystem. However, it is critical to note that the Buddhist notion of selflessness is without grasping, neither a denial of self nor a new attachment on a bigger "non-self". In other words, even altruistic and self-interest sacrificing behaviors could lead to suffering if we fail to understand the transcendent meaning of selflessness.

Chapter Summary

- Wisdom (Pāli: *paññā*) in Buddhism is the ability to understand everything in this world, both internal and external of ourselves, truly, as it is.
- The doctrine of dependent arising states that "when this exists, that comes to be; with the arising of this, that arises … when this does not exist, that does not come to be; with the cessation of this, that ceases."
- It means that nothing arising from nothing, nothing arises from a single condition, nothing arises as a single conditioned factor. It is always the case that from a multiplicity of conditions arise a multiplicity of conditioned factors.
- Strictly speaking, "dependent" means "co-dependent", and "arising" means "co-arising". It is "the middle doctrine".
- We experience the material world (Pāli: *rupa*) through the five senses of sight, hearing, smell, taste, and touch. Together with mental activities, our physical and mental events can be attributed to the five 'aggregates' or 'groups' (Pāli: *khandha*-s).
- Five *khandha*-s (Pāli) are (1) materiality (Pāli: *rupa*), (2) feelings (Pāli: *vedanā*), (3) perceptions/recognition (Pāli: *saññā*), (4) volitional 'forces' or 'formations' (Pāli: *saṃkhāra*), and (5) self-consciousness (Pāli: *viññaṇa*)

- Five aggregates of grasping: not static entities but five constantly changing aspects of individual existence, which always interact with the external world.
- Four kinds of problematic and erroneous clinging: (1) clinging to sense pleasure (Pāli: *kāma-upādāna*), (2) clinging to speculative views on the nature of the self and the world (Pāli: *diṭṭhi-upādāna*), (3) clinging to rites and observances as a means to salvation (Pāli: *sīlabbata-upādāna*), and (4) clinging to a doctrine of self (Pāli: *attavāda-upādāna*).
- Self as a permanent, truly existent identity can be born of (1) delusion (Pāli: *moha*) or ignorance (Pāli: *āvijjā*)—the failure to perceive the world as it actually is; or (2) craving (Pāli: *taṇha*) and attachment (Pāli: *upādāna*)—the desire to identify
- Self: identify with our experiences, apart from our experiences, different from our experiences?
- Construction of self is not only at the conscious and intellectual level, but also at a deep psychological and emotional level, eventually crystallizes at the final stage called conceptual proliferations.
- Once the ego-consciousness has arisen, it cannot exist in a vacuum: it needs ontological support. This process of identification takes the following forms: "this is mine", "this I am", and "this is my self", these forms are respectively arising due craving, conceit, view.
- Self has many forms: the duality between the self and the body; and the identity of self and the body. The Buddhist idea of non-self is based on the denial of both versions.
- Notwithstanding the stability and continuity in us that is built upon causality, it is not permanent.
- What is impermanent is suffering; what is suffering is non-self.

Study Questions

- How is Buddhist wisdom different from intelligence or knowledge?
- How is the notion of "self" established and supported by the five aggregates?
- What is the difference between "dependence" and "co-dependence"?
- Is Buddhist theory of dependent arising deterministic? Or is it random?
- Why is the twelve-factored formula a good illustration of the dependent arising?

Suggested Essay Topics

- Doctrine of dependent arising
- Doctrine of selflessness
- Clinging to the five aggregates and the notion of self
- Twelve-factored formula of dependent arising
- The relationship among Buddhist concepts of dependent arising, selflessness, impermanence, and suffering

Bibliography

Online Multimedia

Thich, Nhat Hanh. 2010. Exclusive Interview with Oprah. Plum Village. Last modified 28 May 2010. https://plumvillage.org/thich-nhat-hanh-interviews/oprah-talks-to-thich-nhat-hanh/

Required Reading

Cantwell, Cathy. 2010. The Three Trainings: III Wisdom. In *Buddhism: The Basics*, 86–90. London/New York: Routledge.

Gethin, Rupert. 1998. No Self: Personal Continuity and Dependent Arising. In *The Foundations of Buddhism*, 133–162. Oxford: Oxford University Press.

Further Reading

Bodhi, Bhikkhu. 2000. *The Connected Discourses of the Buddha, a Translation of the Saṃyutta Nikāya*. Somerville: Wisdom Publications.

CDB. SN 12.1. Nidānasaṃyutta (Connected Discourses on the Causation), Paṭiccasamuppāda Sutta (Dependent Origination). In *CDB*, 533–534. Somerville: Wisdom Publications.

Karunadasa, Yakupitiyage. 2001. *The Early Buddhist Teaching on the Practice of the Moral Life*. The Numata Yehan Lecture in Buddhism Fall 2001, University of Calgary.

———. 2015a. *Early Buddhist Teachings: The Middle Position in Theory and Practice*. Hong Kong: Centre of Buddhist Studies, The University of Hong Kong.

———. 2015b. The Role of Meditation in the Threefold Scheme of Buddhist Mental Culture. In *Buddhist Meditative Praxis: Traditional Teachings & Modern Applications*, ed. K.L. Dhammajoti, 117–122. Hong Kong: Centre of Buddhist Studes, The University of Hong Kong.

MLDB. MN 102. Pañcattaya Sutta: The Five and Three. In *MLDB*, 839–846. Somerville: Wisdom Publications.

MLDB. MN 109. Mahāpuṇṇamā Sutta: The Greater Discourse on the Full-Moon Night. In *MLDB*, 887–891. Somerville: Wisdom Publications.

MLDB. MN 39. Mahātaṇhāsankhaya Sutta: The Greater Discourse on the Destruction of Craving. In *MLDB*, 349–361. Somerville: Wisdom Publications.

Ñanamoli, Bhikkhu, and Bhikkhu Bodhi. 1995. *The Middle Length Discourses of the Buddha: A Translation of the Majjhima Nikaya (Teachings of the Buddha)*. Somerville: Wisdom Publications.

CHAPTER 8

Interconnectedness, Competition, and Collaboration

Beyond Competition: An Collaborative Model of Sustainable Development

In this interconnected world, a unique contribution of Buddhist Economic world-view is the doctrine of dependent arising which promotes win-win collaboration in lieu of self-interest based competition. As discussed in Chap. 7, the principle of dependent arising offers a profound understanding of the relationship between cause and effect. To illustrate the amazing nature of interdependence and the true meaning of interbeing, the *Avataṃsaka Sūtra* uses the metaphor of Indra's Jeweled Net. If we look closely at any one of the jewels on the net, we can see the reflections of all other jewels on its surface. In the reflections of the other jewels we can see the original jewel and the reflections it carries once again being reflected, constituting an infinite interweaved web of reflections. Thich (1997) explains:

> The *Avataṃsaka Sūtra* is the sutra that helps us to see that one element is made of all other elements, and that the all is made of the one. When you look at A, you see B, C, D, E, F, G, H… . When you see B, C, D, E, F, G, H in A, you see everything in A, you see [that] A is not A, [and] that is why A is really A.

With the advancement of technology and global information exchange, decision-makings from one corner of the world could have worldwide implications. However, many decision-makers and leaders still operate and

E. C. H. Ng, *Introduction to Buddhist Economics*,
Studies in Buddhist Economics, Management, and Policy,
https://doi.org/10.1007/978-3-030-35114-4_8

think with a "silo mentality," assuming that they can isolate their self-interest and decision-making processes from rest of the world. Driven by the pursuit of profit or utility, market economy promotes competition and measures success and growth in monetary terms. It seems to cultivate a vicious cycle in which everyone "expect[s] the worst from others" and "produce[s] an enormous abundance of goods and services but at an intolerable environmental and social cost" (Tencati and Zsolnai 2010). Market economy is often called as "dismal science" with a negative connotation of human self-interested nature (Fig. 8.1).

Buddhist Economics emphasizes "interconnectedness." It requires our actions to be non-violent and hence requires us to not cause harm and suffering to ourselves or others (Zsolnai 2007). As Welford (2007) argues, business "is not a 'black box' of activities, but rather part of a network of complex and mutually beneficial arrangement." It "can and should make a difference

Fig. 8.1 *Buddha*-s in mutual respect. Note: Cave 125 of Bingling Temple Grottoes, Gansu, PRC., depicting Gotama *Buddha* and *Prabhūta-ratna* in mutual respect. (Source: Photo by author)

to all people connected with that business, whether that is a businesses' staff or people to be found down supply chain." Tencati and Zsolnai (2010) propose a collaborative model where "good behavior and good expectations reinforce each other" in a virtuous circle. Driven by the goal of creating mutually satisfying relationships with the stakeholders, participants in this model care about each other and themselves and aim to create values for all the participants in the business ecosystems. Counteracting the vicious cycle is the increasing importance of positive psychology studies that research positive subjective experiences, positive individual traits, and positive institutions (Seligman and Csikszentmihalyi 2000). These studies give weight to other human strengths and virtues, as well as necessary interventions, that could support sustainable happiness (Seligman et al. 2004).

As Tencati and Zsolnai (2010) explain, positive research approaches the pursuit of happiness through (1) positive emotion and pleasure, (2) life engagement, and (3) meaning. This approach requires more involvement on the individual's part and demands character strengths from each individual to explore "something larger and more permanent than the self." It also involves development in six areas of virtues: (1) wisdom and knowledge: creativity, curiosity, open-mindedness, love of learning, perspective; (2) courage: authenticity, bravery, persistence, zest; (3) humanity: kindness, love, social intelligence; (4) justice: fairness, leadership, teamwork; (5) temperance: forgiveness, modesty, prudence, self-regulation; (6) transcendence: appreciation of beauty and excellence, gratitude, hope, humor, religiousness.

Following the same line of thought, another approach to the model of economic man (*homo economicus*) is the *homo reciprocans* model in behavioral and social science. In contrast with *homo economicus* assumed by market economy who are exclusively self-interested and always maximize in their utility functions, *homo reciprocans* tend to "cooperate and share" and "respond to cooperative behavior by maintaining or increasing his or her level of cooperation" (Tencati and Zsolnai 2010). Extending this *homo reciprocans* model to the corporate level, research by Frank (2004) indicates that socially responsible firms can survive in competitive environments because they are rewarded for their higher cost: (1) avoid opportunistic behavior between owners and managers, (2) induce employees to work more for lower salaries by moral satisfaction, (3) recruit high quality new employees, (4) gain customers' loyalty, and (5) establish the trust of subcontractors. Tencati and Zsolnai (2010) believe that at the micro level, innovative enterprises can embrace collaboration by "creating values for the different constituencies through creativity, broad stakeholder engagement and more balanced and democratic mechanisms of governance." To ensure the sustainability and competitiveness of a collaborative model, it is also important to tap into the social capital by connecting local communities with the corporates. They believe that a collaborative model will help build a boarder network at the industry and sector level to long-term sustainability and survival issues and eventually build strong public-private partnerships by integrating corporates with political and public entities.

Collaborative model does not ignore the positive contribution of competition in economic activities. The problem is the over-reliance on competition as the "only criterion to rule economic and social life" and putting it as the goal instead of the means. We should evaluate whether competition and innovation are acceptable by "motive"—whether they are driven by the mutually destructive desire to eliminate other competitors or virtuous cycle to enhance productivity to give back to society. Capitalism has an innate creative destructive force where innovations could lead to economic distress or elimination of the non-innovators. Pryor (1991) thinks that a Buddhist economy would embrace innovations if the intention is good and beneficial to the public, the monks and the low-income. Otherwise one should beware of the negative implications on nature, society and future generations in the name of efficiency and competition. Through collaboration and other forms of economic progressive economic models, it is possible to go beyond competition to operate within ecological and social limits (Tencati and Zsolnai 2010).

Dāna: The Practice of Giving

Competition is about winner takes all while collaboration envisions a give-and-take but mutually beneficial relationship. In Buddhist philosophy, the practice of giving (Pāli: *Dāna*) can be identified with "quality of generosity (Pāli: *cāga*)." Even though it is not part of the Noble Eightfold Path, nor is it one of the requisites of enlightenment (Pāli: *bodhipakkhiyā dhammā*), it is one of the essential attributes of the good or superior person (Pāli: *sappurisa*), along with such other qualities as faith, morality, learning and wisdom (Bodhi 2011).

Buddhist teachings devote special attention to the psychological basis of giving. The practice of giving is not simply the transfer of objects from one individual to another. It is "the inward disposition to give." Generosity originates from the motive of renunciation, the thought of eliminating one's attachments to one's possessions and gradually weakens one's craving—a major cause of unhappiness (Bodhi 2011). It is therefore the best weapon against greed (Pāli: *lobha*) and stinginess (Dhp v.221-223). Hoarding wealth beyond our basic needs for future consumption or reinvestment is harmful (Payutto 1998) because it fuels our desire for material possessions, leaving valuable resources idle not for the benefit of the owners or other sentient beings.

To take the initiative to donate, one must understand contentment. Contentment is the realization of what our essential needs are, beyond which we should be satisfied and then divert what we do not need to others. Dhammasami (2003) argues that "[for a lay Buddhist], wealth must be made and used as a beneficial instrument, not a detriment, in the process of achieving enlightenment." It is the understanding of necessity and luxury and no attachment. The *Buddha* says contentment is the highest wealth (Dhp v.202-204), while desire is like fire. Endless competition and desire to win at all cost is like a fierce fire which must be quenched off by collaboration.

Buddhism considers an intelligent donation is comparable to a rewarding investment in a field of merits, not an expense. Through donation, positive thoughts such as generosity, selflessness, and understanding of the wisdom behind possession are cultivated. Instead of wasting our blessings, we "recycle" and "redistribute" the conditions contributing to our wealth for the benefit of others without any expectation or attachment. One who gives is a man with faith (Pāli: *saddhā*); he has faith in the nobility of a morally sound life, in the teachings of *kamma* (Pāli) and survival after death. He believes in the possibility of moral and spiritual perfection in man. In short, he is not a materialist and has faith in the *Buddha*, the *dhamma* and the *saṅgha* (Bodhi 2011).

Even if we give simply in hopes of winning luxury in our future lives, we may still attain our goal provided that we adhere to the principles of virtuous conduct (Bodhi 2011). A gift made with the desire for pleasure is accompanied in part by the unwholesome psychological root of craving (Pāli: *taṇhā*). However, if we aspire to ultimate peace and purity by practicing generosity, we will develop the perfection of giving (Pāli: *dānapāram*), building up a store of merit that will bear its full fruit with our attainment of enlightenment (Pāli: *nibbāna*) (Bodhi 2011).

In addition to the motivation behind giving, the recipients of the gifts are also important. The *Buddha* teaches that the worthiest recipients of gifts are the noble ones with pure minds attained by wisdom. The noble ones are therefore also regarded as the field of merits—just as seeds sown in fertile well-watered fields yield bountiful crops, alms given to the virtuous established on the Noble Eightfold Path yield fruitful results (NDB. AN 3.57 and 8.34). The *saṅgha* is described as "an unequalled field of merit-making for the world" (Pāli: *anuttaraṃ puññakkhettaṃ lokassa*) (Bodhi 2011). The *Dakkhiṇāvibhaṅga Sutta* (MN 142.9–13) states that an offering is purified on account of the giver when the giver is virtuous, on account of the recipient when the recipient is virtuous, on account of both the giver and the recipient if both are virtuous, by none if both happen to be impious (Bodhi 2011).

The third factor involved in giving is the gift itself (Bodhi 2011). Giving is threefold by way of the object to be given: (1) the giving of material things (Pāli: *āmisadāna*), (2) the giving of fearlessness (Pāli: *abhayadāna*), and (3) the giving of the *dhamma* (Pāli: *dhammadāna*). Among these, the object to be given can be twofold: internal and external. The external gift is tenfold: (1) food, (2) drink, (3) garments, (4) vehicles, (5) garlands, (6) scents, (7) unguents, (8) bedding, (9) dwellings, and (10) lamps. The internal gift should be understood in two ways. Just as a man, for the sake of food and clothing, surrenders himself to another and enters into servitude and slavery; in the same way the Great Man, wishing for the supreme welfare and happiness of all beings, desiring to fulfill his own perfection of giving, with a spiritually-oriented mind, for the sake of enlightenment, surrenders himself to another and enters into servitude, placing himself at the disposal of others (Bodhi 2011).

The most common type of gift is material things, but they need not have a high monetary value to bring great results. The *Buddha* taught about eight great gifts which have been held in high esteem by the noble ones (NDB. AN 8.39). Their value was not doubted in the past, present, and future. The wise recluses and Brahmins had the highest respect for them. These great gifts comprise the three refuges to the *Buddha*, the *dhamma*, and the *saṅgha*, and the meticulous observance of the Five Precepts (abstaining from the destruction of life, abandoned the taking of what is not given, abstains from sexual misconduct, abstains from false speech, abstains from liquor, wine, and intoxicants). By doing so one gives fearlessness, love and benevolence to all beings. If one human being can give security and freedom from fear to others by his behavior, then that is the highest form of *dāna* one can give, not only to mankind, but to all living beings (Bodhi 2011).

The giving of the *dhamma* (Pāli: *dhammadāna*) is a honorable discourse on the *dhamma* given with an undefiled mind—that is, methodical instruction conducive to good in the present life, to good in the life to come, and to ultimate deliverance (Bodhi 2011). By means of such discourses, those who have not entered the *Buddha*'s release enter it, while those who have already entered it reach maturity therein—"A gift of Dhamma conquers all gifts" (Dhp v.334-359).

Bodhisatta is the exemplary donor as he gives in this manner whenever the opportunity presents itself, strictly in order to fulfill the "perfection of giving" (Pāli: *dānapārami*). A *Bodhisatta* must give more difficult gifts than material goods to fulfill the highest form of the perfection of generosity. He must freely give away the most precious gift for normal humans, such as parts of his body, his children, his wife, and even his own life (Bodhi 2011).

Wake Up Together: From Personal Development to Social Development

In the maximizing principle of the market economy, we indulge in consumption and spending without reflecting that humans and our planet Earth are in grave danger. Our present ways of living have caused great harm to the ecosystem, increasing income inequality, and increasing stress and social pressure. Through market operations, we disengage from our responsibility to society and the environment. We fail to properly and equally reflect the interests of those who are not represented such as our future generation, other non-human members of the environment, the less influential like low-income and disadvantaged groups and so forth. Yet we continue to live in oblivion as if business as usual. Thich (2010) calls for a collective awakening:

> In my mind I see a group of chickens in a cage disputing over a few seeds of grain, unaware that in a few hours they will all be killed … We can't continue to live like this. It's not a sustainable economy … We have to have another dream: the dream of brotherhood and sisterhood, of loving-kindness and compassion. That dream is possible right here and now … Mindfulness is at the heart of awakening, of enlightenment.

The problems humans face are so overwhelming, we may end up being frustrated by entrenched thinking and rigidity in established institutions of vested interests and bureaucracies. There is no doubt that the way humans interact with the environment is not sustainable. However, we should not be despair because we have the wisdom and the dharma (Thich 2010). In our daily lives, there are always changes we want to see to improve our personal and societal situations. Many of us are eager to make changes in the workplace and in society. We desire to live in peace and harmony in a sustainable environment. We are convinced that there are better initiatives to leverage the strength of market institutions to better serve human well-being. Instead of blaming the government or corporate institutions, we should organize ourselves and wake up together. The missing links are urgent, concrete, and proactive action at the individual and collective levels to make a strong commitment to sustainable living a reality (Thich 2010):

> It's time for each of us to wake up and take action in our own lives. We have the power to decide the destiny of our planet. If we awaken to our true situation, there will be a change in our collective consciousness. We have to do something to wake people up.

Moral cultivation at the individual level is uniquely important in Buddhist Economics because "one who is stuck in the mud of moral depravity cannot save another who is in the same predicament. One who has pursued one's own moral well-being is in a sure position to help others to pursue their own moral well-being" (Karunadasa 2015). Thus, moral cultivation has an individual as well as a social dimension. In actuality, when it comes to the practice of moral life, the very distinction between our own good and the good of others tends to be obliterated.

Presumably everyone desires happiness and disliking pain, so there is no good reason to add to the common lot of suffering. The benefit of self and others are intertwined, so that concern to lessen one's own suffering goes hand-in-hand with lessening that of others. "One who pursues one's own moral good is morally good, but one who pursues one's own moral good as well as others' moral good is morally better" (Karunadasa 2015). Helping others helps oneself (through karmic results and developing good qualities of mind), and helping oneself (by purifying one's character) enables one to help others better.

In response to the collective action required to drive change for better environmental protection, Thich suggested that "we need a real awakening, enlightenment, to change our way of thinking and seeing things" (Confino 2012). This real awakening is to move beyond talking about humans and the environment, or in another context, opposing conceptualizations of you and me, high-income and low-income, individuals and society, and so forth, because these polarized mindsets lead people to think of two separate confronting entities. It is only possible to deliver change when we transcend these dichotomic views and see the two as one and the same. To be truly sustainable as a business, a family, an organization, or a religion, all stakeholders need to stay together and walk together. For a community of practitioners to practice together, it requires a shared vision and a shared path. We need to share good fortune and bad fortune. Without this sense of commonality, the very fundamental value of democracy supporting the market economy would be shaken (Sandel 1998). The *Buddha* proclaimed that there is a path leading to the cessation of suffering, liberation, and hence sustainable happiness. This "old path white clouds" has been walked by all the noble ones. This contemplative journey is not an easy one, but the *Buddha* and his students invite everyone to "walk with me."

Bhikkhu Bodhi argued: "Two dimensions of our lives [i.e. the internal and the external, the personal and the social] are inseparably intertwined and mutually conditioning, so that our values reflect social and economic realities, while social and economic realities are shaped by our values [at the individual level]. Thus, while it is in our personal lives that we have the most power to instigate direct change, any alternations in our personal lifestyles must also reach outwards and exercise an impact on our interpersonal relations, our social order, our political agenda, and our relationship to the natural environment" (Bodhi 2000).

Box 8.1 To Compete or to Collaborate, That Is the Question...
Market economic theories justify competition with the assumption of scarcity but ignoring the nature of human coordination and cooperation (North 1990). Leaders with great political and financial influence must realize the great responsibility they carry. They demonstrate a lack of humility and a lack of awareness of the interconnected nature of individuals, society, and nature, and show the failure to realize the adverse consequences of self-interested acts. For example, when the US withdrew from The Paris Agreement in 2017,

(*continued*)

Box 8.1 (continued)

previously agreed on by 195 countries in 2015, they should have acknowledged the time, effort, and compromises it took for so many nations to put a workable agreement together. When President Trump mentioned that no deal would be better than a bad deal, he is still thinking with a win-or-lose mindset, in which he is only willing to be the winner in every situation, and if he has to lose, this would only be acceptable in a lose-lose situation. This way of thinking is driven not only by self-interest but also desire and delusion. Similarly, as we can see with the global financial crisis, Brexit, presidential and general elections in the UK and the US, as well as the decision of the US to leave Trans-Pacific Partnership and Paris climate accord, there is a dangerous trend of politicians and financial market participants gambling for some marginal wins for "one" at the expense of "all."

Dalio (2017) has voiced concern at how the increasing number of conflicts has a detrimental effect on the government and the economy. Dalio elaborated that he is inclined to analyze Trump's policies, as a global and US citizen, from an economic and market-oriented perspective, which is further informed by a thorough study of history and nature, and an understanding of the patterns of cause and effect. He was alarmed by the observation that: "When faced with the choices between what's good for the whole and what's good for the part, and between harmony and conflict, [Trump] has a strong tendency to choose the part and conflict."

To some extent, Dalio shares a Buddhist understanding of the concept of interdependence as he "believe[s] that we are connected to our whole ecology, our whole world community, and our whole United States, such that it pays to be in symbiotic relationships with them" (Dalio 2017). He is thus concerned about Trump's path of conflict and particularly the impact this path might have on his presidency and rest of the world.

When this path of conflict and hostility is paved with the desire for an absolute "win" at the expense of the "other," a hatred toward those who are not part of "us," and delusion of the independent nature of this world and of nature, we should all share this concern.

Chapter Summary

- Market economy promotes competition and measures success and growth in monetary terms. It cultivates a vicious cycle where everyone "expect[s] the worst from others."
- It puts overreliance on competition as the "only criterion to rule economic and social life" and glorifies "economic competition as an end in itself", even though the achievements are made at the expense of nature, society and future generations.
- A collaborative model proposes "good behavior and good expectations reinforce each other" in a virtuous cycle. Positive research approaches the pursuit of happiness through (1) positive emotion and pleasure, (2) life engagement, and (3) meaning.
- It is driven by the goal of creating mutually satisfying relationships with the stakeholders, people care about each other and themselves with the aim to create values for all the participants in the business ecosystems.
- Instead of assuming humans as an economic man (*homo economicus*), *homo reciprocans* tend to "cooperate and share" and "respond to cooperative behavior by maintaining or increasing his or her level of cooperation."
- Collaboration would require more involvement on the individual's part and demands character strengths from each individual to explore "something larger and more permanent than the self."
- Practice of giving can be identified with "quality of generosity (Pāli: *cāga*)" and it is one of the essential attributes of the good or superior person (Pāli: *sappurisa*), together with other qualities as faith, morality, learning and wisdom.
- Practice of giving is not simply the transfer of objects from one individual to another. It is "the inward disposition to give." Buddhist teachings devote special attention to the *psychological basis of giving*.
- Offering is purified on account of the giver when the giver is virtuous, on account of the recipient when the recipient is virtuous, on account of both the giver and the recipient if both are virtuous. The motivation behind giving and the recipients of the gifts are both important.
- There are three kinds of giving: (1) the giving of material things (Pāli: *āmisadāna*), (2) the giving of fearlessness (Pāli: *abhayadāna*), and (3) the giving of the *dhamma* (Pāli: *dhammadāna*).

- *Bodhisatta* is the exemplary donor as he gives in this manner whenever the opportunity presents itself, strictly in order to fulfill the "perfection of giving" (Pāli: *dānapārami*).
- Thich calls for a collective awakening: "the dream of brotherhood and sisterhood, of loving-kindness and compassion…is possible right here and now. We have the Dharma, we have the means, and we have enough wisdom…"
- Benefit of self and others are intertwined. The good wish to lessen one's own suffering goes hand-in-hand with lessening that of others. Moral cultivation has an individual as well as a social dimension.

Study Questions

- What are the *pros* and *cons* of competition?
- Is competition the driving force or the necessary element of market economy?
- Is human inherently competitive or collaborative?
- Why is a collective awakening impossible?
- How could change be possible even when top-down solutions are not available?
- What is the difference between the gift and the "inward disposition to give"?
- What are the three types of gift and which is more precious than the other? Why?

Suggested Essay Topics

- Buddhist doctrine of interconnectedness and collaboration
- Collaboration and competition in market economy
- *Dāna* and the Buddhist practice of giving
- Three types of Buddhist giving and their meanings
- Collective awakening: individual and social moral cultivation

Bibliography

Online Multimedia

Parker, Ceri. 2019. New Zealand Will Have a New 'Well-Being Budget,' Says Jacinda Ardern. World Economic Forum. Last modified 23 January 2019. https://www.weforum.org/agenda/2019/01/new-zealand-s-new-well-being-budget-will-fix-broken-politics-says-jacinda-ardern

Required Reading

Bodhi, Bhikkhu. 2011. *Dāna: The Practice of Giving: Selected Essays*. Second 2003 ed, The Wheel Publication No. 367–9. Kandy: Buddhist Publication Society. Reprint, 2005, online edition 2011. http://www.bps.lk/olib/wh/wh367.pdf

Tencati, Antonio, and László Zsolnai. 2010. Beyond Competitiveness: Creating Values for a Sustainable World. In *The Collaborative Enterprise: Creating Values for a Sustainable World*, ed. Antonio Tencati and László Zsolnai, 375–388. Oxford: Peter Lang Academic Publisher.

Further Reading

Bodhi, Bhikkhu. 2000. *Facing the Future: Four Essays on Buddhism and Society*. Kandy, Sri Lanka: Buddhist Publication Society.

———. 2012. *The Numerical Discourses of the Buddha: A Translation of the Aṅguttara Nikāya*. Translated by from the Pāli by Bhikkhu Bodhi. Somerville: Wisdom Publications.

Confino, Jo. 2012. Beyond Environment: Falling Back in Love with Mother Earth. *The Guardian*, 20 February 2012, Guardian Sustainable Business. http://www.theguardian.com/sustainable-business/zen-thich-naht-hanh-buddhidm-business-values

Dalio, Ray. 2017. The Last 24 Hours' Developments in the UK and US Increase the Odds That Conflict Will Lead to Political Ineffectiveness. *LinkedIn*, 9 June 2017. https://www.linkedin.com/pulse/last-24-hours-developments-uk-us-increase-odds-conflict-ray-dalio

Dhammasami, Khammai. 2003. Can a Buddhist Be a Wealthy Man? *Shap Journal* XXVI (2003/2004): 28–29.

Dhp. v.202-204. Sukhavagga: Happy. (Dhp XV), Translated from Pāli by Thanissaro Bhikkhu. *Access to Insight*. Last modified 30 November 2013. http://www.accesstoinsight.org/tipitaka/kn/dhp/dhp.15.than.html

Dhp. v.221-234. Kodhavagga: Anger. (Dhp XVII) *Access to Insight*. Translated from Pāli by Thanissaro Bhikkhu. Last modified 30 November 2013. https://www.accesstoinsight.org/tipitaka/kn/dhp/dhp.17.than.html

Dhp. v.334-359. Tanhavagga: Craving. (Dhp XXIV) *Access to Insight*. Translated from Pāli by Thanissaro Bhikkhu. Last modified 30 November 2013. https://www.accesstoinsight.org/tipitaka/kn/dhp/dhp.24.than.html

Frank, Robert. 2004. *What Price the Moral High Ground? Ethical Dilemmas in Competitive Environments*. Princeton: Princeton University Press.

Karunadasa, Yakupitiyage. 2015. *Early Buddhist Teachings: The Middle Position in Theory and Practice*. Hong Kong: Centre of Buddhist Studies, The University of Hong Kong.

NDB. AN 3.57. Vaccha. In *NDB*, 254–256. Somerville: Wisdom Publications.

NDB. AN 8.34. The Field. In *NDB*, 1166–1168. Somerville: Wisdom Publications.
NDB. AN 8.39. Stream. In *NDB*, 1173–1175. Somerville: Wisdom Publications.
North, Douglass C. 1990. *Institutions, Institutional Change and Economic Performance*, 1990. New York: Cambridge University Press.
Payutto, P.A. 1998. *Buddhist Economics, a Middle Way for the Market Place*. Bangkok: Buddhadhamma Foundation.
Pryor, Frederic L. 1991. A Buddhist Economic System. In Practice: The Rules of State Policy Making of the Ideal King's Sought a "Middle Way" Between Right and Left. *American Journal of Economics and Sociology* 50 (1): 17–32.
Sandel, Michael J. 1998. *What Money Can't Buy: The Moral Limits of Markets*. Tanner Lectures on Human Values, Brasenose College, Oxford, May 11 and 12, 1998.
Seligman, Martin E., and Mihaly Csikszentmihalyi. 2000. Positive Psychology: An Introduction. *American Psychologist* 55 (1): 5–14.
Seligman, Martin E., Acacia C. Parks, and Tracy Steen. 2004. A Balanced Psychology and a Full Life. *Philosophical Transactions: Biological Sciences* 359 (1449): 1379–1381.
Thich, Nhat Hanh. 1997. *The Diamond Sutra*. Transcript of the Dharma Talk Given by Thich Nhat Hanh. 14 December 1997 in Plum Village. http://www.abuddhistlibrary.com/Buddhism/G%20-%20TNH/TNH/The%20Diamond%20Sutra/Dharma%20Talk%20given%20by%20Thich%20Nhat%20Hanh%20on%20December%2014%20IV.htm
———. 2010. The Bells of Mindfulness. In *Moral Ground: Ethical Action for a Planet in Peril*, ed. Kathleen D. Moore and Michael P. Nelson, 79–81. Texas: Trinity University Press.
Welford, Richard. 2007. Examining, Discussing and Suggesting the Possible Contribution and Role of Buddhist Economics for Corporate Social Responsibility. *International Journal of Green Economics* 1 (3/4): 341–350.
Zsolnai, László. 2007. Western Economics Versus Buddhist Economics. *Society and Economy* 29 (2): 145–153.

PART V

The Path

CHAPTER 9

Envisioning a Different "Growth Model"

Less Is More: Frugality

While market economy focuses on a maximizing principle with more is more, there are also other economic models which propose alternative perspective of less is more, small is beautiful, and a minimizing principle. One of these models is frugality which is a conception of the good life with a "deep philosophical and religious roots in the East and the West" (Bouckaert et al. 2011). It is not the same as "stinginess" but an *art de vivre*—the art of living which opens up our minds for spiritual goods with low material consumption and a simple lifestyle.

The Greek philosopher Epicurus, one of the pioneers in frugality thinking, developed a rational theory and ethics of frugality which can be further understood through two principles on the ethics of sustainable enjoyment. The first principle argues that frugality is a rational assessment. Since pleasure is less clear and less certain, while pain, anxiety, and confusion are prominent, obvious, and direct, the pursuit of pleasure makes sense when pain, anxiety, and confusion are reduced. According to Epicurus, frugality is necessary to reach the highest form of pleasure *ataraxia*—or imperturbability—a state in which the soul is not disturbed, just like the sea is calm and undisturbed by the wind. The second principle is the simplification of our needs because we suffer when our greater desires are not met. We fail to enjoy our lives because we tend to "seek short-time gain rather than durable and last-

E. C. H. Ng, *Introduction to Buddhist Economics*,
Studies in Buddhist Economics, Management, and Policy,
https://doi.org/10.1007/978-3-030-35114-4_9

ing satisfactions." We waste our energy on illusionary or indoctrinated needs at the expense of basic human needs.

Frugality is not only relevant on a personal level, but also on a macro socio-economic system level. For example, Max-Neef (1991) attempts to rethink poverty and wealth based on a deeper understanding of human nature. In his framework, human needs can be categorized into nine areas: (1) subsistence, (2) protection, (3) affection, (4) understanding, (5) participation, (6) idleness, (7) creation, (8) identity, and (9) freedom. These human needs have to be satisfied at the four existential modes: (1) being, (2) having, (3) doing, and (4) interacting—altogether forming a thirty-six/nine-by-four complex system of satisfiers. An important implications from this framework of human needs are that societies and individuals can be dysfunctional not only when they have too little, but also when they have too much economic goods—"The world is not divided between the 'haves' and the 'have-nots' but between a majority that do not have enough and a minority that has too much" (Bouckaert et al. 2011). Frugality in this context is the ability to realize what are the essential material resources and economic goods necessary to satisfy all basic needs in a given situation, putting economic goods as the means to serve the end of "healthy (holy) living and interacting" (Bouckaert et al. 2011).

Nevertheless, the motivation behind frugality can affect the results. If we adopt frugality as a rational instrument or a tactic to save more, invest more to satisfy our desire to be wealthier or happier in the future, we will become even greedier and less happy. As Bouckaert, Opdebeeck and Zsolnai (2011) explain, this will crowd out the intrinsic meaning of frugality:

> As a rational concept, frugality is an enlightened but ego-centered relation to our environment. In the spiritual traditions, frugality gets another meaning. Its first meaning is about self-detachment, a release from the active, self-seeking ego.

The spiritual practice of frugality can be achieved without falling into a severe form of ascetics. In spiritual traditions, it illustrates enormous potential of compassion and solidarity between the "haves" and "have nots" in society. The practice of compassionate frugality, on both the individual and the institutional level, will gain strength if it is supported by a sense of ecological interconnectedness beyond rational calculation (Bouckaert et al. 2011). The spiritual and rational motivations of frugality are intertwined. The spiritual motivation is often hidden behind a rational narrative and vice versa. As illustrated below (see Box 9.1), there are good examples of *spiritual homo economicus* among for-profit or non-profit entrepreneurs and business leaders. Their profiles comprise those who are market-oriented, efficient, and driven by genuine social and ecological spirituality. Spiritually based frugal practices do not necessary contradict self-interest based rational calculation (Bouckaert et al. 2011).

Box 9.1 Less Is More: Slow Food Movement and Trappist Brewery of Westmalle Examples

To counteract the rise of mass scale fast food chain operations, the Slow Food movement was founded in the 1989 to promote local food cultures and traditions, encouraging consumers to be more interested in "the food they eat, where it comes from and how are food choices affect the world around us." The movement is now a global initiative with millions of supporters in over 160 countries. As opposed to consuming more and more food at a fast pace generating more and more food waste, the movement invites consumers to reflect on the relationship between food and various aspects of life such as culture, politics, agriculture, and the environment, with the objectives of influencing how "food is cultivated, produced and distributed, and change the world as a result." It envisions a world in which "all people can access and enjoy food that is good for them, good for those who grow it and good for the planet ... good clean fair food for all" (Slow Food 2019).

The Trappist Brewery of Westmalle in Belgium is an interesting example of *spiritual homo economicus*. The tradition has a history of over two centuries, and it has been positioned "not as a purely economic activity, but rather, it is a service to the community." It has a spiritual bottom line expressed in the charter of the brewery. In observance of the Rule of St. Benedict, the key elements of this charter are (i) small scale, (ii) deep ecological respect, (iii) work as a spiritual value, (iv) product quality, not pricing strategy or advertising, should determines the choice of the consumer, and (v) sharing profit (Trappist Westmalle 2019 and Bouckaert 2008). It is part of a "special economy". Revenues the brewery should support the cost of living of the abbey, factoring into other human and environment costs, as well as supporting people in need.

Steady-State Economy: Economics in a Full World

In market economy, most humans and social problems seem to be resolvable by growth. Daly (2005) responded that it might be possible only if the global economy existed in a vacuum independent of the finite biosphere supporting it. He urges that humans to recognize and avoid "uneconomic growth," which produces "bads" faster than goods, increasing costs by more than it increases benefits—making us poorer instead of richer. This endless pursuit of growth results in relatively less money and time invested in basic needs, such as caring for one's family, the eradication of poverty, ecological maintenance, and so forth. Moreover, the income disparity between different social groups widen and people become increasingly disconnected with the rest of society (Bouckaert et al. 2011). Recognizing and avoiding uneconomic growth is not easy because people with vested interested may resist change. In addition, many aspects of "uneconomic growth" are not measurable or manifested within a short period. Transition to a sustainable economy demands a radical change in mindset of many stakeholders with vested interests.

Daly (2005) believes that humans must make this transition to a sustainable economy, which can operate long term by observing the inherent biophysical limits of the global ecosystem. Otherwise we are exposing ourselves not only to uneconomic growth but also ecological catastrophe that harms our well-being. This concern for sustainability is definitely not new: John Stuart Mill in the 1850s discussed and welcomed a *Stationary State*, Schumacher (1984), and Georgescu-Roegen (1971) continued the discussions on evolutionary and ecological economics in the 1960s and 1970s. In view of the limits of the ecosystem, any subsystem including the economy, must at some point stop growing in a dynamic equilibrium like a steady state.

At the microeconomic level, people consider the trade-off between marginal cost and benefit and stop when the marginal cost equals marginal benefit (Daly 2005). But at the macro level, there is no meaningful discussion on how trade-offs among people, material goods, natural resources, generations. Economic theory has traditionally dealt with allocation instead of determining the sustainable scale. We do not know when to stop and how to address this new scarcity in a "full world" economics (Daly 2005).

Therefore, we must specify what is to be sustained from year to year: are we aiming at sustainable growth in GDP, "utility," *throughput*, natural capital, or total capital (the sum of natural and man-made capital)? Stop growing GDP, according to Daly (2005), does not mean stop developing. While GDP growth may not be sustainable, development can be. Qualitative improvements which increase GDP could still be achievable without increasing the amount of resources used. Sustainability of "utility" is challenging because utility is difficult to measure, translate or transfer over time. Natural resources, in contrast, are things that can be measured and transferred. If we can truly understand production as the mere change from one impermanent state to another: from coal to power to manufactured goods, we would realize all economic activities have costs in terms of both inputs, desirable outputs and undesirable outputs—productivity is not possible without our valuable time, labor, fuel, a forestry, clean water supply, fresh air or even the life of other animals or human beings. Hence sustainability could be understood in the terms of *throughput* instead (Bouckaert et al. 2011), based on the human, societal, and environmental capacity for supplying each raw resource and for absorbing the end waste products (Daly 2005) (Fig. 9.1).

Fig. 9.1 Envisioning a mindful economy. Note: The author led a mindfulness hike on the subject of mindful economy at European Forum Alpbach. (Source: Photo by author)

The problem with "efficiency first" is that improvement can be made with an even larger consumption of the factor which efficiency has increased. The price of that factor declines and more uses for the cheaper factor are found. The net result is that there is even greater scale of consumption of the resource than before, even if it is produced more efficiently (Bouckaert et al. 2011). While "efficiency first" does not induce frugality, a focus on overall *throughput* with a policy of "frugality first" can result in the obtainment of efficiency as a secondary effect. Daly (2005) argues that we should focus on limiting *the scale of the economy* relative to the ecosystem by restraining uneconomic growth. The total amount of *throughput* allowed can be achieved with a *cap-and-trade* system, considering the capacity of the environment to regenerate resources or absorb pollution.

It is not safe to assume that new technology will always loosen limits imposed by the ecosystem (Daly 2005). Schumacher (1984) argues that Buddhist Economics emphasizes the role of humans "as if people mattered." If economic activities are meant to serve people and the environment, any adoption of technology should be "appropriate," in a way that it will not undermine our engagement in work and creativity. Without wisdom, technology will only mean a greater concentration of economic power, and violence against the environment. Technology may increase productivity, but not necessarily contribute to our well-being and happiness. In the market economy, it has been frequently developed and applied to manipulate and stimulate our greed, excitement, and delusions, instead of relieving stress, alleviating mental distress and disorders, or contributing to inner peace and tranquility.

Buddhist teachings in mindfulness and interdependence would cautious us against being attached, manipulated, or even enslaved by new technology. Humans are supposed to have the "choice" of letting go of or unplug from technology if they choose. New technology, particularly that in the digital age (internet, social media, artificial intelligence, and so forth) can become so integrated with every part of human lives as if it is invisible. Ironically, if technology can anticipate and cater for our desires, making sure that our wishes are always fulfilled, we may no longer be truly free. It is important to reflect what make us human and how we could stop feeding the technology innovation that we cannot control.

Box 9.2 Envisioning a Sustainable Economy (Daly 2005)
Product lifetimes: a "demographic transition" of people and goods in a way production rates should equal depreciation rates although the steady level could be varied.

GDP growth: still achievable even with a constant throughput with the support of efficiency and qualitative advancement even with constant throughput.

Financial sector: interest rates are expected to fall with lower growth and inflation. Investments are made for replacement and upgrade instead of speculative bubbles.

Trade: free trade would not be feasible between sustainable and unsustainable economies because the former will demand fair trade with proper pricing on costs associated with other social and environmental factors.

Taxes: instead of taxing the value added such as salary, income, or profit, government would tax the throughput flow (that to which value is added) to encourage more efficient resource use.

Employment: promote more local and labor-intensive employment to support maintenance and repair instead of new production.

Happiness: societies that have reached sufficiency, sustainability should mean limited sacrifice on happiness.

Small Is Beautiful: Right Livelihood Based on Buddhist Ideals

Schumacher (1984) explains that Buddhist Economics differs from the market economy as it sees "the essence of civilization not in a multiplication of wants but in the purification of human character." Buddhist Economics considers consumption and economic growth to be optimal when it manages to satisfy a high degree of human needs by a relatively low rate of consumption, without putting too much pressure on living a good life and a moral life. Building upon a simple and non-violent economic relationship, it does not aim at pursuing an endless growth—"the marvel of the Buddhist way of life is the utter rationality of its pattern—amazingly small means leading to extraordinarily satisfactory results." Buddhist Economics is conscious of the deep implications in choosing between local and imported products, renewable and non-renewable materials, and so forth. Schumacher (1984) believes that it could be recommended "even to those who believe that economic growth is more important than any spiritual or religious values." The question is not a choice between modernity over tradition, growth over stagnation. It is about "the right path of development, the Middle Way between materialist heedlessness and traditionalist immobility, in short, of finding 'Right Livelihood'".

In Buddhist teachings, right livelihood as in the Noble Eightfold Path is an integral part of spiritual and personal development—work is important and essential in and of itself (Schumacher 1984). The market economy considers work as something to get rid of, to be reduced, or to be enhanced with division of labor and ultimately automated. It means that work is not a good thing. In Buddhist Economics, right livelihood would mean work in compliance with the five precepts of no manufacturing or trading in weapons, no trading in living beings (the slave trade and prostitution), in meat, in intoxicants, and in poisons (Halkias 2013). Material wealth should not be a cause for attachment and craving but serve as the conditions to support spiritual development.

In Buddhist Economics, work has at least three important functions: (1) to give man a chance to utilize and develop his faculties; (2) to enable him to overcome his ego-centredness by joining with other people in a common task; and (3) to bring forth the goods and services needed for a becoming existence (Schumacher 1984). Work is a valuable opportunity to build character and will bless those who do it as well as their products. Without work, one would be in a desperate situation, not only financially but also spiritually because he lacks the "nourishing and enlivening factor of disciplined work". Kumarappa (1957) expounds that if the importance of work could be fully appreciated:

> It nourishes and enlivens the higher man and urges him to produce the best he is capable of. It directs his free will along the proper course and disciplines the animal in him into progressive channels. It furnishes an excellent background for man to display his scale of values and develop his personality.

Accordingly, two types of work which must be clearly distinguished: (1) one that enhances a man's skill and power and (2) one that turns the work of man over to a mechanical slave, leaving man in a position of having to serve the slave. Focusing on productivity and growth would indicate a preference of goods over people and consumption over creative activity. In contrast, Buddhism is the middle way supportive of both physical and mental well-being: "It is not wealth that stands in the way of liberation but the attachment to wealth; not the enjoyment of pleasurable things but the craving for them" (Schumacher 1984).

In the consumption-based economy, our purchasing decisions are often more driven by desires than needs. While most people all have basic requirements to keep their body and mind nourished with food, clothing, and shelter, the desires for design, beauty, and quality are manifestations of their self-gratification. Yet these objects of desire often appear on everyone's list of "must-haves". Some of us may have so many extra appliances, utensils, gadgets, items of clothing, and so on, even when these excess things are rarely used and when the basic needs of the underprivileged groups in the communities are not met. Consumers are confused about their real happiness (what we really feel) with whether their perceived happiness (others' perception) and how many means they possess to become happy. In this way, consumption, possessions, career, and wealth could define human identity to an extent that many of us risk our identity when we lose what we manage to consume and produce. Humans could, in the worst case, lose their self-esteem and mental stability when they go bankrupt or lose their jobs.

Buddhism calls these attachments, as humans are bonded and dragged by their consumption and production activities in the process. Recognizing how people gain security and self-recognition with their possessions, humans should be smart about what they need instead of what they desire. Necessities of life are easier and more stable to maintain instead of a luxurious way of life. Buddhism introduces right consumption, meaning consumption of the right objects with moderation and contentment. It reminds us to focus on the present and inward developments—mind and body—instead of focusing on the external world, such as the relationship with one's spouse, family, colleagues, or even more challenging, the consumption of alcohol, drugs or sex. Buddhism distinguishes between true happiness from the means of happiness and perceived happiness. Without moderation, consumption will lead to attachment as humans focus on the chase, like a relationship between a predator and prey. Consumers, being the predators, think they are in control of the pursuit. In reality, they are being led and dragged by their desires when unavoidably following every move of the prey. It is indeed a paradox in the consumer economy that consumers prefer more choices, but too much choice stresses them out (Schwartz 2004)—it is not only difficult to decide what to buy, but it is also difficult to decide what to consume after some impulsive purchases. Making choices could be much easier if humans can keep things simple.

Box 9.3 Minimalism
To keep things simple, minimalist movement has as a lifestyle has been a topic of much interest over the last few years. Joshua F. Millburn & Ryan Nicodemus led a minimalist movement for nearly a decade which promotes a focus on "getting past the things so that we can make room for life's important things—which aren't *things* at all." It does not focus on having less but "making room for more: more time, more passion, more creativity, more experience, more contribution, more contentment, more freedom. Clearing the clutter from life's path helps make that room." This awareness and change lead us to happiness (Minimalism 2019).

Another thought leader in minimalism is Marie Kondo, a Japanese "decluttering" and "organizing" consultant who advocates managing our belongings and possessions by methodically gathering them together, one category at a time, then holding on only to those that "spark joy" in our lives. Each of our possessions should serve a function and we don't need to own multiple sets of them, says Kondo: "the items we decide to keep should each occupy a designated place in our home so that we can easily find and make good use of them."

Another prominent voice in the minimalist movement is Hideko Yamashita, who teaches the practice of *dan-sha-ri*, which means to "refuse" unnecessary new purchases, "dispose" of existing clutter, and "separate" oneself from the desire for material possessions.

Chapter Summary

- Frugality is not stinginess but an *art de vivre*—the art of living which opens up our minds for spiritual goods with low material consumption and a simple lifestyle.
- Greek philosopher Epicurus developed a rational theory and ethics of frugality as a rational assessment and the simplification of our needs.
- Frugality has a macro socio-economic implication: The world is not divided between the "haves" and the "have-nots" but between a majority that do not have enough and a minority that has too much.
- Motivation behind frugality can affect the results. Compassionate frugality on the individual level as well as the institutional level will gain strength if it is supported by a sense of ecological interconnect-

edness beyond rational calculation. The spiritual and rational motivations of frugality are intertwined.

- Market economy seems to suggest that most problems can be resolved through growth. Daly urges us to recognize and avoid "uneconomic growth," which produces "bads" faster than goods—making us poorer, not richer.
- Relative poverty of some groups becomes worse and these groups will feel increasingly disconnected with the rest of society. Economic theory has traditionally dealt with allocation instead of determining the sustainable scale.
- *Spiritual homo economicus* and frugality can be integrated in corporate scenarios.
- Sustainability: need to specify what is to be sustained from year to year: are we aiming at sustainable growth in GDP, "utility", throughput, natural capital…?
- While GDP growth may not be sustainable, development can be. Sustainability should be understood in the terms of throughput.
- While "efficiency first" does not induce frugality, a focus on overall throughput with a policy of "frugality first" can result in the obtainment of efficiency as a secondary effect.
- Market economy considers "work" as something "to get rid of." It means that work is not a good thing. Buddhist teachings emphasize work and "right livelihood" as spiritual and personal development.
- Buddhist Economics sees "the essence of civilization in the purification of human character." Simplicity and non-violence are inseparable. Optimal consumption manages to satisfy human needs by a low rate of consumption, not sacrificing a good life and a moral life.

Study Questions

- Is Buddhist's notion of Small is Beautiful the same as Minimalism?
- Is *Less is More* or *More is More?*
- Does de-growth or no-growth mean poverty?
- Is frugality or minimalism spiritual or rational?
- Are there any good examples of frugality, minimalism, and *spiritual homo economicus*?

Suggested Essay Topics

- Frugality and income disparity
- Small is beautiful and minimalism
- Frugality
- Less is more
- Uneconomic growth and sustainability
- Frugality and minimalism as a rational or a spiritual response to market economy
- Perspectives of Buddhist Economics in frugality and minimalism
- Case studies on frugality, minimalism, or *spiritual homo economicus*

Bibliography

Online Multimedia

D'Avella Matt. 2015. *Minimalism: A Documentary About the Important Things*. Netflix. https://www.youtube.com/watch?v=0Co1Iptd4p4

Marie Kondo. 2019. *Tidying Up with Marie Kondo*. Netflix. https://www.youtube.com/watch?v=WvyeapVBLWY

Required Reading

Bouckaert, Luk, Hendrick Opdebeeck, and Lászlo Zsolnai. 2011. Frugality. In *The Palgrave Handbook of Spirituality and Business*, ed. Luk Bouckaert and László Zsolnai, 269–276. London: Palgrave Macmillan.

Daly, Herman E. 2005. Economics in a Full World. *Scientific American*. (Nature Publishing Group) 2005 (September): 100–107.

Further Reading

Bouckaert, Luk. 2008. Rational Versus Spiritual Concepts of Frugality. In *Frugality: Rebalancing Material and Spiritual Values in Economic Life*, ed. Luk Bouckaert, Hendrik Opdebeeck, and László Zsolnai, 27–43. Oxford: Peter Lang Publishers.

Georgescu-Roegen, Nicholas. 1971. *The Entropy Law and the Economic Process*. Cambridge: Harvard University Press.

Halkias, Georgios T. 2013. The Enlightened Sovereign; Buddhism and Kingship in India and Tibet. In *A Companion to Buddhist Philosophy*, ed. Steven M. Emmanuel, 491–511. Oxford: Wiley-Blackwell.

Kumarappa, Joseph C. 1957. *The Economy of Permanence*. Varanasi: Sarva Seva Sangh Prakashan.

Max-Neef, Manfred. 1991. *Human Scale Development. Conception, Application and Further Reflections.* New York: Apex Press.
Minimalism. 2019. https://www.theminimalists.com/about/#the_mins. Last accessed 28 Aug 2019.
Schumacher, Ernst F. 1984. *Small Is Beautiful: Economics as if People Mattered.* London: Sphere Books Ltd. Original edition, 1973.
Schwartz, Barry. 2004. *The Paradox of Choice: Why More Is Less.* New York: Ecco, HarperCollins Publishers.
Slow Food. 2019. https://www.slowfood.com/. Last accessed 28 Aug 2019.
Trappist Westmalle. 2019. The Vision of the Monks of Westamalle on Brewing. https://www.trappistwestmalle.be/en/vision-monks-westmalle-brewing. Last accessed 28 Aug 2019.

CHAPTER 10

Alternatives to Profit-Driven Economic Growth Models

Sustainability: Long Term Versus Short Term

Sustainability refers to "the preservation of a particular state of existence" (Kovács 2014). In 1987, the World Commission on Environment and Development Report defined sustainable development as "development that meets the needs of the present without compromising the ability of future generations to meet their own needs" (World Commission on Environment and Development 1987). It focuses on the concept of needs particularly for the low-income groups and the technological and social, organizational constraints on meeting such present and future needs. With the rise of the market economy, financial crises and economic instability seem to be not only unavoidable but also ever more widespread and detrimental when economies across the world become more integrated.

Internationally, the United Nations Millennium Development Goals ("MDGs") were signed in 2000 by all the 191 United Nations member states to try to achieve by the year 2015. It attempted to address the concept of "needs" and assist the development of underdeveloped countries. There are eight main goals: (1) the eradication of extreme poverty and hunger; (2) the achievement of universal primary education; (3) the promotion of gender equality and the empowerment of women; (4) the reduction of child mortality; (5) the improvement of maternal health; (6) combating HIV/AIDS, malaria, and other diseases; (7) securing environmental sustainability; and (8) the development of a global partnership (MDG 2019).

E. C. H. Ng, *Introduction to Buddhist Economics*,
Studies in Buddhist Economics, Management, and Policy,
https://doi.org/10.1007/978-3-030-35114-4_10

The MDGs were later redesigned into the seventeen Sustainable Development Goals ("SDGs"). These are the blueprint to achieve a better and more sustainable future for all by 2030 (SDG 2019). These goals comprise (1) no poverty; (2) zero hunger; (3) good health and well-being; (4) quality education; (5) gender equality; (6) clean water and sanitation; (7) affordable and clean energy; (8) decent work and economic growth; (9) industry, innovation, and infrastructure; (10) reduced inequities; (11) sustainable cities and communities; (12) responsible consumption and production; (13) climate action; (14) life below water; (15) life on land; (16) peace, justice, and strong institutions; and (17) partnerships.

Kovács (2014) compares the approaches of the MDGs with the Buddhist one by looking into the MDGs, the Threefold Training, and its eight divisions. He argues that the MDGs' focus on basic necessities resonates with the Buddhist emphasis on food, clothing, shelter, and medical care. However, the eight MDGs could go beyond basic needs into higher living standards and development areas such as (1) human capital, (2) infrastructure, and (3) human rights (social, political, and economic). Indeed, some of these shortfalls were also being addressed in the design of the 17 SDGs above. Kovács (2014) also maintains the perspectives of some Buddhist Economics scholars, which focus on the instrumental value of these development goals to support the Buddhist ultimate development goal of spiritual perfection and liberating the mind. He also criticizes MDGs for their relative lack of discussion on the concrete policies or actions to achieve these goals while Buddhist frugal, simple, environmentally sound livelihood could ensure environmental sustainability.

The ultimate goal of Buddhism is not material sustainability, but spiritual perfection. After satisfying basic necessities, a Buddhist lifestyle encourages inner development through the Middle Way or the Threefold Training. Material development on its own is discouraged and unimportant above a necessary level for one's inner advancement. Sustainability emerges as a *by-product* of the ongoing purification of the human character rather than a goal to be striven for.

From Gross National Product to Gross National Happiness

Buddhism believes happiness is more than sensory pleasure derived from physical comfort. It is an innate state of mind that can be cultivated through spiritual practice, overcoming mental and emotional states which induce suffering. Economic indicators like Gross National Product ("GNP"), however, typically measure a society's well-being in terms of material productivity development. Under GNP, only functions with measurable monetary value are important. The more we consume and invest, the happier we are, thus correlating state of well-being with material consumption and investment. This may encourage waste because more outputs under the GNP calculation need to be produced even at the expense of other outputs (such as waste) that are not calculated under the GNP. Yet the exploitation of natural resources is not calculated as an economic loss. Since material goods are limited, we view other people as competition for limited resources. Such an incredibly narrow vision of economic growth fails to distinguish between healthy or unhealthy growth, temporary or sustainable growth. Short-term rewards become more important than long-term, sustainable investments. The future is compromised because any resources of value to future generations are heavily discounted. Similarly, if money can be made and economic activities can operate without intangible values such as moral virtues, the market seems to discount their cultivation heavily (Fig. 10.1).

Fig. 10.1 Bhutan, the Kingdom of GNH. Note: The author presented at the Seventh International Conference on Gross National Happiness at Thimphu, Bhutan. (Source: Photo by author)

Gross National Happiness ("GNH") is one of the new economic indices that has emerged in the wake of these revelations. To measure the collective happiness of a nation, it builds upon four pillars: (1) economic development, (2) good governance, (3) cultural preservation, (4) nature conservation. Still, measuring happiness is hard since so much of life is non-quantifiable. The most common approach is directly asking people how they feel, but those results are superficial because short-term sensory happiness is then mistakenly equated with deeper inner experiences. A better approach is measuring the phenomena that make people happy and unhappy (Tideman 2004).

Intangible values are equally important as material goods for our well-being. Over the last decades, immaterial and non-monetary factors have been gaining more recognition and importance in economic models. For example, "Compassionate Economy" focuses on the informal, unpaid economy of caring, sharing, nurturing of the young, volunteering, and mutual aid, which account for around 50% of all productive work and exchange in all societies. However, it has been traditionally ignored by economic statistics and GNP calculations (Tideman 2004). Ethics and morals are in fact the underlying foundation of markets (Smith 1817). There are values and human pursuits which are not for sale but are the most essential ones to make us human: justice, freedom, worship, leisure, family, charity, and love (Kuttner 1997). Happiness is not purely determined by what we have or how much we consume, but "also by what we know, how we can manage, and how we can be creative, ultimately by who we are—so not by having, but by being" (Tideman 2004). Recent research on stress shows that people who seek only short-term pleasure are more prone to stress than those who seek a higher purpose. Medchikov (2009) observes that:

> most people are not really maximizers, but what one might call "satisfy-ers": they want to satisfy their needs, and that means being in equilibrium with one self, with other people, with society, with civilization, and with nature …it is a basic equilibrium. And it's also reflected in the family. The relations within the family are mostly based on altruism and compassion.

Spiritual traditions advise us to make altruism the core of our practice, not only because it is the cheapest and most effective insurance for our future, but because it will bring about a transformation of the mind. Compassion and non-monetary values, not commodities, will make us happy. In contrast, the never-ending pursuit of happiness in the form of material goods will lead to suffering: we fear we will lose out; we fear our desires will not be fulfilled. The *Buddha* teaches these emotions are based on ignorance and a misconception of reality, and can be removed by the understanding of reality. By sharing with others, the level of competition may not be as intense as we fear by realizing that we are mutually dependent on each other's success. Goleman (1995) has shown that at least 30% of the company's performance can be attributed to its corporate culture—success in business heavily depends on the quality of cooperation among colleagues.

Buddhist teachings suggest that happiness can be achieved by evolving our consciousness from self-interested to selflessness, from an independent *silo* mindset to that of interdependent. It is a state of mind or consciousness, and the mind and consciousness are distinct from "things". The Middle Way school proposed by Nagarjuna would argue that both mind and matter exist, not independently but interdependently on each other. Payutto's (1998) perspective on the market in the Middle Way focuses on moderation and non-harming, striking a balance between material and spiritual pursuit in all three interconnected aspects of human beings, society, and the natural environment. While Newton, Descartes, and classical economics define the world in things, separate building blocks, the doctrine of selflessness, and dependent arising introduced earlier suggest that no one thing exists independent of another. Focusing on only "things" blindfolds humans from appreciating the complex relationship and context giving rise to the "things" and the implications of our decision-making. Yet our spiritual developments are also dependent on material support. This mutual dependency also applies to GDP and GNH (Tideman 2004). Focusing on GDP alone ignores the higher potential of humankind, but without food and shelter, people cannot focus on developing themselves spiritually. GDP could serve as the lowest-level "bottom line", while GNH comprises the whole spectrum of values. GNH ultimately represents a balance of mind and matter, market and government, self-organization and planning, opening up and retaining control, compassion and competition. It could serve as "a balancing act between mind/matter, market/government, self-organization/planning, opening up/retaining control and compassion/competition", and it should "transcend these black and white notions by recognizing the fundamental interconnectedness of all things" (Tideman 2004).

The environmental and social costs of development, such as pollution and destruction of air, water, forests, and other supposedly "free goods", have recently been given more weight as well. There should be more attention over how common goods are priced, used, and allocated. We should be aware of the high risk imposed on ourselves and the system if we ignore corporate responsibility and sustainability. We should go beyond financial bottom line to research, report, and manage our double (financial and social impact) or triple (social, environmental, and financial) bottom line exposures.

There are models which attempt to integrate GDP and GNH. These models include (1) Phuntshok, Prakke, and Chettri (1999) efforts to tie the Noble Eightfold Path of Buddhism together with the value-based psychology of Maslow and Bhutan's GNH components; and (2) the seven levels of consciousness (service, making a difference, internal cohesion, transformation, self-esteem, relationship, and survival) developed by Barrett (2013) based on inspiration from Maslow and Vedic principles as cultural transformation tools. Tideman (2004) believes that these seven levels of consciousness could be linked to the Noble Eightfold Path, Hierarchy of Needs of Maslow (1943), as well as the "four pillars" definition of GNH.

Box 10.1 Measuring Well-Being

Apart from GNH, there are similar indexes such as the Calvert-Henderson Quality of Life Indicators (Henderson et al. 2000) which represent the national comprehensive effort in the United States to redefine overall quality of life using a systems approach with 12 quality life indicators in (1) education, (2) employment, (3) energy, (4) environment, (5) health, (6) human rights, (7) income, (8) infrastructure, (9) national security, (10) public safety, (11) recreation, and (12) shelter. The US Misery Index was first developed to calculate the relationship between economic indicators (sum of unemployment and inflation) and well-being. It was later modified to include other economic factors such as unemployment rate, bank lending rates, and the real GDP per capita in the calculation.

Brown and Sällström (2019) have developed a Sustainable Shared-Prosperity Policy Index (SSPI) to measure policies that support a meaningful life in a sustainable world. There are almost 50 policy indicators in three board categories: (1) policies that structure markets with rules and taxes; (2) measures to protect the environment; and (3) government programs that support healthy, educated people along with the infrastructure and human rights that establish a well-functioning society.

Sufficiency Economy

Sufficiency is another important element in the strategies for sustainability, besides efficiency and consistency. It is not about suppressing our desires or abandoning material wealth but knowing what is enough. It is about "how to deal with our wealth, how to satisfy our desires more deeply and how to enjoy a qualitatively better life by consuming less" (Bouckaert et al. 2011). Similar to minimalist movement, sufficiency is an alternative model of being present and conscious with our consumption countering the vicious cycle of working harder and consuming more.

Sufficiency Economy as an economic model is proposed in Thailand by King Bhumibol Adulyadej. It serves as an antithesis to the "scarcity and deficiency" in consumerism and competition, short-term gain and exploitation, amassing more and more wealth without limitation or consideration for non-monetary factors. It is rooted in the principle of morality and contentment that if people are satisfied with their needs, then they will crave for less, and with less craving and greed, there will be less suffering. Buddhism teaches that our lives progress in a way that involves a harmonious balance between the internal causes within our own life (our personality, experiences, outlook on life, etc.) and the external conditions and relations around us. Through applying this philosophy of interdependence and the Middle Way of moderation and enough in our daily lives, we will realize that the modern life of excessive material gains is flawed. It is an economic model driven by virtues instead of greed and lack of morality (Punyaboon 2014).

At the individual level, Sufficiency Economy allows people to build a firm base of self-reliance and see that the true meaning of happiness lies in being satisfied with ourselves. At the corporate level, it helps them take "corporate responsibility to the next level." For government and its relevant sectors, it serves as a guide to alleviating poverty, promoting good governance, and guiding macroeconomic policies to immunize against shocks in this globalized economy. In a Sufficiency Economy, self-sufficiency and happiness are achieved by maintaining a balance in five areas including (1) state of mind, (2) social affairs, (3) natural resources and the environment, (4) technology, and (5) economic affairs (Punyaboon 2014). Its core principles are moderation, reasonableness, self-immunity, wisdom, and integrity. The United Nations Development Programme (2007) explained that (1) moderation could be best understood in terms of the Middle Way, enough but transcending above not too little and not too much, "between want and extravagance, between backwardness and impossible dreams"; (2) reasonableness in terms not of rationality, but the ability to understand the implications of our actions and hence compassion; (3) self-immunity in terms of "resilience", and "the ability to withstand" against external shocks and uncontrollable events. These principles could be best served with the required conditions of wisdom and integrity. Knowledge or wisdom means the accumulated knowledge and insight to make good decisions, and integrity is the moral discipline including honesty, tolerance, diligence, and non-exploitation.

While emphasizing its potential contribution to sustainable development, the Sufficiency Economy does not mean economic independence or economic self-sufficiency. It could apply to people or entities with different value systems, even if they strongly believe in growth (Punyaboon 2014). It should also be applicable to countries without a Buddhist background although Buddhist knowledge would help deepen its meanings (Essen 2010).

Implementing Changes at Different Levels: Individual, Social, and Environmental

In Buddhism, human suffering is caused by defiled states of mind and unskillful human actions whose origin is greed (Pāli: *lobha*), hatred (Pāli: *dosa*), and ignorance (Pāli: *moha*). These unwholesome actions and states expand beyond the individual and contaminate society and the country at large. The role of the Buddhist community is to ensure that policy-making aligns with the *dhamma* and that the ruler is a just one who works for the welfare and harmony of the community.

The *Cakkavattisīhanāda Sutta* (LDB. DN 26) identifies poverty as the origin of social vices and crime. In the *Kūṭadanta Sutta* (LDB. DN 5), the *Buddha* taught that it is unwise to spend and waste national wealth on festivities and celebrations because, eventually, people will be burdened by extra taxes necessary to restore the fiscal budget after these wasteful activities. State leaders must be "aware and conscious of" the actual situation of the economy to properly deploy resources necessary for the economic process. Crime and social disorder due to low-income economic policies would not be stopped by fines or punishments. Instead, leaders of the state should conserve resources and allocate them to society in the form of support such as capital, seeds, and equipment to engage in economic activities to contribute to their well-being. It is when members of society could follow each of their own businesses that society could be prosperous and harmonious:

> Then those people, being intent on their own occupations, will not harm the kingdom. Your Majesty's revenues will be great, the land will be tranquil and not beset by thieves, and the people, with joy in their hearts, will play with their children, and will dwell in open houses. (LDB. DN 5)

This *sutta* suggested that Buddhism proposed "not mere mass scale employment of people, but the use of human resources in a planned manner in keeping with the totality of the economic structure, so that labor so utilized will contribute to the enhancement of total production" (Nanayakkara 1995). Buddhism encourages coordinated planning of the whole economic structure, which involves selection of areas that require government aid, the type of aid required, and the proper utilization of such aid.

The ruler should possess certain virtues (*dasa-raja-dhamma*). This is important not just because a ruler must lead by example, but also because the doctrine of dependent arising suggests that people can have an effect on their environment by both their physical actions and their moral conduct. Failure to act according to the *dhamma* will bear karmic retributions to the kingdom, the people, and the king himself. On the other hand, spiritual merit (*paññā*) can be gained by following Buddhist teachings (Halkias 2013).

Wiltshire also notes that if the monarch does not rule according to the *dhamma*, he loses the right to be king. Buddhism absorbs the notion of "power" wholly into the notion of "ethical justice"; the former cannot thrive without the latter (Wiltshire 1990). One particular chapter of the *Ratnavali*, attributed to the second-century Indian philosopher Nagarjuna, shows how the king is counseled on how to rule his kingdom based on Buddhist principles (Halkias 2013). These balancing forces "limits the potential despotism of the state and its subordination to the dhamma makes it an instrument of morality; hence, the state becomes a moral institution" (Gokhale 1953).

Instead of pure self-interest or utilitarian considerations, Zsolnai (2009) established that a decision-maker's set of choices is largely determined by his or her perceived responsibility. In other words, the decision-maker would consider what one "ought to" or "should" do so that one would be responsible, largely in term of moral responsibility, for both the individual and organizations (Zsolnai 2009). Being responsible means we are actors responsible for (1) our actions, (2) socially expected actions associated with certain roles, or (3) the way actors evaluate and decide on different choices available in the context of decision-making. For human beings, it could also mean a responsibility in relation to the continuation of human life and the natural environment, either as a result of natural responsibility as a parent or as a contractual responsibility as a statesman.

The Responsible Decision Making Model comprises three "Rs", which are (1) rationality in goal achievement, (2) reverence for the applicable ethical norms, and (3) respect for the affected stakeholders (Zsolnai 2009). In another formulation, Zsolnai (2011) criticized market economy for using profit as the sole measure of rightness in decision-making and motivation. He proposed that economic activities should take into account other more significant reasoning, such as ecological, future-respecting, and pro-social considerations.

Chapter Summary

- Sustainable development is development that meets the needs of the present without compromising the ability of future generations to meet their own needs.
- Internationally, the United Nations' eight Millennium Development Goals (MDGs) and seventeen Sustainable Development Goals are initiatives aiming at the sustainable well-being of humans, society, and the environment.
- Buddhist teaching is fundamentally about the eradication of suffering from the basic human needs like food, clothing, shelter, and medical care, to higher spiritual developments. Buddhism believes happiness is more than sensory pleasure derived from physical comfort.
- GNP typically measures a society's well-being in terms of economic growth, that is, material gains. It assumes that only commodities with monetary value are important, and the main human impulses are competition and consumption.
- Buddhist and other sustainable economic models focus on mutual dependency of both values and material developments. These two are both important and not mutually exclusive.

- Sufficiency Economy is rooted in the principle of contentment and has its basis in the understanding that if people are satisfied with their needs, then they will crave for less; and with less craving and greed, there will be less suffering.
- It aims at a harmonious balance between the internal causes within our own life (our personality, experiences, outlook on life, etc.) and the external conditions and relations around us. It allows people to build a firm base of self-reliance and see that the true meaning of happiness lies in being satisfied with ourselves.
- Unwholesome human actions and states of mind could expand beyond the individual and contaminate society and the state at large.
- The *Cakkavattisīhanāda Sutta* identifies poverty as the origin of social vices and crime. In the *Kūṭadanta Sutta*, the *Buddha* recognizes that crime cannot be reduced through harsh punishments, but can only be eliminated through sound plans of economic development.
- Individuals can have an effect on their environment through their physical actions and their moral conducts. Zsolnai proposes a responsible decision-making model that is accountable to individuals, the society, and the environment. It comprises the three "Rs" of rationality, reverence, and respect.

Study Questions

- What is sustainability? How is it being manifested in the MDGs, SDGs, and GNH?
- How are material and spiritual needs, or GNP and GNH, related?
- How is Sufficiency Economy related to Buddhist Economics?
- What is responsible decision-making?
- How is responsibility defined?

Suggested Essay Topics

- Sustainability and happiness
- Gross National Product and National Happiness
- Spirituality and values in developments
- Sufficiency Economy and Buddhist Economics
- Leveraging changes at different levels: individual, societal, and environmental
- Responsible decision-making and business ethics

Bibliography

Online Multimedia

de Botton, Alain. 2016. How to Improve Capitalism. In *The School of Life*. https://www.youtube.com/watch?v=YOaJe68C-bU&index=50&list=PLwxNMb28XmpehnfQOa4c0E7j3GIj4qFEj

UN SDGs. 2019. Do You Know All 17 SDGs? In *United Nations Sustainable Development Goals*. https://youtu.be/0XTBYMfZyrM

Required Reading

Kovács, Gábor. 2014. *Buddhist Approach to Sustainability and Achieving Millennium Development Goals*. The 11th of International Buddhist Conference on the United Nations Day of Vesak (2014/2557), Cat Bai Dinh Temple, Ninh Binh, Vietnam.

Punyaboon, Rachroat. 2014. Sufficiency Economy: An Innovative Method of Buddhist Development Economics. *Journal of Humanities and Social Sciences* 3 (2): 33–54.

Tideman, Sander G. 2004. *Gross National Happiness: Towards a New Paradigm in Economics*. First International Conference on Operationalization of Gross National Happiness, Bhutan, Thimphu.

Further Reading

Barrett, Richard. 2013. *Liberating the Corporate Soul—Building a Visionary Organization*. London/New York: Routledge.

Bouckaert, Luk, Hendrick Opdebeeck, and Lászlo Zsolnai. 2011. Frugality. In *The Palgrave Handbook of Spirituality and Business*, ed. Luk Bouckaert and László Zsolnai, 269–276. London: Palgrave Macmillan.

Brown, Clair and Simon Sällström. 2019. What America Needs to Understand About Capitalism. *Project Syndicate*. Last modified 12 July 2019. https://www.project-syndicate.org/commentary/america-presidential-election-reform-capitalism-by-clair-brown-and-simon-sallstrom-2-2019-07

Essen, Juliana. 2010. Sufficiency Economy and Santi Asoke: Buddhist Economic Ethics for a Just and Sustainable World. *Journal of Buddhist Ethics* 17 (2010): 69–99.

Gokhale, Balkrishna G. 1953. Dhammiko Dhammaraja: A Study in Buddhist Constitutional Concepts. In *Indica*, 161–165. Bombay: St. Xavier's College.

Goleman, Daniel. 1995. *Emotional Intelligence*. New York: Bantam Books.

Halkias, Georgios T. 2013. The Enlightened Sovereign; Buddhism and Kingship in India and Tibet. In *A Companion to Buddhist Philosophy*, ed. Steven M. Emmanuel, 491–511. Oxford: Wiley-Blackwell.

Henderson, Hazel, Jon Lickerman, and Patrice Flynn, eds. 2000. *Calvert-Henderson Quality of Life Indicators*. Bethesda: Calvert Group.

Kuttner, Robert. 1997. *Everything for Sale: The Virtues and Limits of the Market*. Chicago: University of Chicago Press.

LDB. DN 5. Kūṭadanta Sutta: About Kūṭadanta: A Bloodless Sacrifice. In *LDB*, 133–141. Somerville: Wisdom Publications.

LDB. DN 26. Cakkavatti-sīhanāda Sutta: The Lion's Roar on the Turning of the Wheel. In *LDB*, 395–405. Somerville: Wisdom Publications.

Maslow, Abraham H. 1943. A Theory of Human Motivation. *Psychological Review* 50 (4): 370–396.

MDG. 2019. *Millennium Development Goals*. United Nations. Last Accessed 28 Aug 2019. https://www.un.org/millenniumgoals/

Medchikov, Stanislav. 2009. Compassion or Competition Forum – Amsterdam Dialogue 1999. In *Compassion or Competition*, ed. Sander Tideman. Amsterdam: Bohn Stafleu van Loghum.

Nanayakkara, S.K. 1995. Social Dimensions of Buddhism. In *Encyclopedia of Buddhism. Extract* No. 3, ed. by W.G. Weeraratne. Padukka: The State Printing Corporation.

Payutto, P.A. 1998. *Buddhist Economics, a Middle Way for the Market Place*. Bangkok: Buddhadhamma Foundation.

Phuntshok, Kenpo, Diederik Prakke, and Sammdu Chettri. 1999. Gross National Happiness: Concepts for the Debate. In *Gross National Happiness: A Set of Discussion Papers*, ed. Sonam Kinga, Karma Galay, Phuntsho Rapten, and Adam Pain, 104–115. Thimphu: Centre of Bhutan & GNH Studies. https://www.bhutanstudies.org.bt/gross-national-happiness-a-set-of-discussion-papers/

SDG. 2019. *About the Sustainable Development Goals*. United Nations. Last Accessed 28 Aug 2019. https://www.un.org/sustainabledevelopment/sustainable-development-goals/

Smith, Adam. 1817. *The Theory of Moral Sentiments*. First American ed. Philadelphia: Anthony Finley.

United Nations Development Programme. 2007. *Thailand Human Development Report: Sufficiency Economy and Human Development*. UNDP, Bangkok. Accessed 1 Dec 2015. http://hdr.undp.org/sites/default/files/thailand_2007_en.pdf

Walshe, Maurice. 1986. *The Long Discourses of the Buddha: A Translation of the Dīgha Nikāya*. Translated by from the Pali by Maurice Walshe. Somerville: Wisdom Publications.

Wiltshire, Martin. 1990. *Ascetic Figures Before and in Early Buddhism: The Emergence of Gautama as the Buddha*. Berlin: Mouton de Gruyter.

World Commission on Environment and Development. 1987. *Our Common Future, from One Earth to One World*. Oxford: Oxford University Press.

Zsolnai, László. 2009. *Responsible Decision Making*. New Brunswick: Transaction Publishers.

———. 2011. Redefining Economic Reason. In *Spiritual Humanism and Economic Wisdom: Essays in Honour of Luk Bouchaert's 70th Anniversary*, ed. Hendrik Opdebeeck and László Zsolnai, 187–201. Antwerpen & Apeldoorn: Garant Publishers.

CHAPTER 11

Making Sustainable Decisions in Daily Life

Moral Discipline: The Five Precepts

There are many schools of Buddhism but all would agree with the Threefold Training of moral discipline, mental concentration, and wisdom. According to Karunadasa (2015a), the Threefold Training are in fact three stages of moral development corresponding to the three levels of expression of unskillful moral qualities: (1) moral discipline, to restrain our morality, expressed in vocal and physical actions; (2) mental concentration, to still the mind in turbulence, although it cannot remove unskillful qualities lying below surface-consciousness; and (3) wisdom, to uproot all roots of moral unskillful qualities which have sunk to the "bottom" of the mind when the mind becomes still. Instead of a quick fix, the practice of a moral life is a graduated discipline (Pāli: ***anupubba-sikkhā***), a graduated course of conduct (Pāli: ***anupubba-cariyā***), and a graduated mode of progress (Pāli: ***anupubba-paṭipadā***) of our mind and bodily actions.

Moral disciplines in Buddhism are the dos and don'ts of a moral life. They are the compasses to direct internal thought processes and external vocal and physical actions (Ng 2018). As discussed in Chap. 2, external acts of transgression due to temptation could be more harmful, but are easier to control than thoughts of temptation themselves. They should, therefore, be the level where the practice of moral life begins (Karunadasa 2001). Moral disciplines ensure harmony in the mental and bodily actions within oneself, but also within a community and should be enacted based

E. C. H. Ng, *Introduction to Buddhist Economics*,
Studies in Buddhist Economics, Management, and Policy,
https://doi.org/10.1007/978-3-030-35114-4_11

on an empirical understanding of human minds and actions and how they affect development. Rules for monastics are generally stricter than what is expected of lay people. Moral disciplines are also foundations for the cultivation of mental concentration and wisdom. While mental concentration can focus and relax minds, without the development of wisdom and moral discipline, one can focus on the wrong subjects with the wrong perspectives. Wisdom without concentration is equally fruitless because our minds wander around without pinpointing on the right subjects (Ng 2018).

The Five Precepts (Pāli: *pañca-sīla*) (LDB. DN 31)—not taking life, not taking what is not given, no sexual misconducts, no lying, no intoxicants—serve as the basis of Buddhist moral practice. They are not commandments, but rather a vow to oneself to respect and observe them. In the Noble Eightfold Path, the five specific trades of wrong livelihood, including trading in weapons, living beings, meat, intoxicants, and poisons, are also in compliance with the Five Precepts (NDB. AN 5.177). Observance of these precepts are the great offerings of freedom from danger, animosity, and oppression to limitless numbers of beings (NDB. AN 8.39). The Five Precepts are drawn from the "three pure precepts": "Cease from evil, do only good, do good for others", as well as the "ten great precepts" that begin the fifty-eight *Bodhisatta* precepts from the *Brahmajāla Sūtra*. Parts of the "ten great precepts" are equivalent to the first four precepts; the remaining six include (5) not taking or selling intoxicating drugs or alcohol, (6) not speaking against others, (7) not praising oneself and abusing others, (8) not being mean in giving *dhamma* or wealth, (9) not being angry, and (10) not defaming the "three jewels" (Harvey 2013).

Buddhism does not encourage strong guilt even if we fail to observe the precept. For an action to break a precept and be karmically harmful, it must be performed with intention. A "Middle Way" is best, avoiding the extremes of laxity and rigidity. Guilt is seen as part of the natural karmic result of unskillful action and indeed the acknowledgment of faults is an important part of monastic training, but only to a certain point. Self-hatred and mental turbulence will only hinder us spiritually. The role of "conscience" is performed by "right mindfulness", which makes one aware of one's actions and motives, along with self-respect (*hiri*) and regard for consequence (*ottappa*). *Hiri* causes one to strive to avoid any action which one feels is not worthy of oneself and lowers one's moral integrity. *Ottappa* is fueled by concern over reproach and blame, embarrassment, legal punishment, or the karmic results of an action.

Box 11.1 Five Precepts

First Precept of Not Taking Life (Harming Living Creatures): considered as the most important, involves the resolution not to intentionally kill any human, animal, bird, fish, or insect. The word for "living being" (*pāna*) in the precept literally means "breather", a living thing that draws air (Harvey 2013). Hence it refers to humans, animal, and all sentient life (Cantwell 2010a).

Second Precept of Not Stealing (Taking What is Not Given): rules out theft, fraud, cheating, gambling, borrowing without the intention to return, and taking more than one's due (Harvey 2013). It refers to any unwilling forms of appropriation of property from others (Cantwell 2010a). It also covers any immoral means to generate wealth and harm imposed on others' possession.

Third Precept of No Sexual Misconduct (Illicit Sex): concerns "misconduct concerning sense-pleasures". This includes adultery, incest, rape, and intercourse with those who are not supposed to (Harvey 2013). It also implies that sexuality should not involve any exploitation or breaking of trust (Cantwell 2010a).

Fourth Precept of No Lying (False Speech): deals with "false speech", is seen as the second most important because a person who feels no shame in intentional lying is capable of any evil action. It is associated with the four aspects of the "right speech" factor (Harvey 2013), that is, false speech, slanderous speech, harsh speech, and idle chatter.

Fifth Precept of No Intoxicants (Leading to Heedlessness): renounces alcoholic drink or toxics that obstruct mindfulness. It differs from the first four precepts in that it does not overtly warn against inherent evil, but helps maintain the other precepts (Cantwell 2010a). One is more likely to break the other precepts and hinder one's ability to develop the right state of mind.

In the Five Mindfulness Trainings, Thich (2009) offers specific guidance and practices, which adhere to the *Buddha*'s vision of the Four Noble Truths and the Noble Eightfold Path with modern interpretations applicable to the modern world. He describes these trainings as "the path of right understanding and true love, leading to healing, transformation and happiness for ourselves and for the world".

(*continued*)

Box 11.1 (continued)

The Five Mindfulness Trainings include (1) reverence for life—awareness of the suffering caused by the destruction of life; (2) true happiness—awareness of the suffering caused by exploitation, social injustice, stealing, and oppression; (3) true love—awareness of the suffering caused by sexual misconduct; (4) loving speech and deep listening—awareness of the suffering caused by unmindful speech and inability to listen to others; and (5) nourishment and healing—awareness of the suffering caused by unmindful consumption.

The prerequisite for making sound decisions is a disciplined way of thinking and action. To cultivate discipline, one should follow the teachings of other achieved predecessors, notably the *Buddha* himself and his teachings. Initially, one should follow the precepts based on a leap of faith in the teacher and his teachings. By acting and reflecting on the precepts diligently and mindfully, we could gradually understand the significance of these precepts and finally internalize them wholeheartedly. By following the precepts, a Buddhist student creates the necessary and sufficient conditions required to focus and develop wisdom from mental activities. In the *Ambalaṭṭhikā-rāhulovāda Sutta* (MLDB. MN 61), the *Buddha* taught *Rahula* to reflect deeply and honestly on our bodily, verbal, and mental actions through repeated reflection. More importantly, in deep self-reflection, the *Buddha* taught *Rahula* to reflect on the consequences of his actions, whether they led to self-affliction, the affliction of others, or both. Alternatively, whether they led to painful consequences, painful results, and so forth. It is through this disciplined reflection that insight is developed by seeing our actions beyond time and space.

Life's problems are no less complex than the mundane problems relating to sustainable economic growth. Responsible decision-makers should similarly integrate moral discipline, mental concentration, and wisdom into the decision-making process. To apply moral discipline, we should first identify a teacher or a role model. We can learn from their positive and negative experiences and develop a set of rules-disciplines conducive to sustainable decision-making. We need to commit to acting and thinking in adherence with our core principles, and avoid actions and thought processes in the opposite direction. This commitment to self-control in our decision-making and actions is necessary because, through a deep self-examination, we will understand situations where we fail to maintain consistent rational decisions in real life. Greed and fear prevent us from sustainable thinking because we crave for what we do not have and fear of losing what we already have. For each decision we make, our views reinforce our identity as the decision-makers, as we recognize the decision made and the "I" capable of making the decision. When good or bad decisions are made, we feel accordingly good or bad about ourselves as a decision-maker. We define ourselves not by the profit generated, but by the decision and action we took to maximize wealth.

To achieve sustainable happiness, decision-making must also abide by moral discipline. It is possible only when our livelihood is consistent with morality and values, so that we do not cause harm or unhappiness to ourselves and others. Moral livelihood is by itself a happy mode of life. Happiness requires us to train our mind to "form habits leading to lasting happiness" through diligent cultivation and maintenance (Chang 2006).

Mental Concentration

Mental concentration (Pāli: *samādhi*), the second out of the Threefold Training, is central throughout mainstream Buddhist traditions. Meditative commitment is sometimes practiced in a retreat or monastic environment with few distractions over a period of years (Cantwell 2010b). As illustrated in the *Sacitta Sutta* (NDB. AN 10.51), a Buddhist practitioner should train his mind with deep self-examination. To make this self-examination fruitful, one must be entirely courageous, honest, mindful, and alert to one's unskillful qualities and be determined to abandon these unskillful qualities.

Different schools have different techniques, but in general, meditative training involves any kind of practice that focuses the mind and deepens awareness. Ideally, the power of emotional afflictions overwhelming the mind could be reduced and an inner experience of tranquility, happiness, and clarity could come about. One important and popular meditation practice is the Four Immeasurables (*Brahmavihāra*) (Cantwell 2010b). In the Eightfold Path, "perfect meditative absorption" is closely associated with tranquility meditation. "Right Mindfulness" is needed as well, though that is more related to the development of insight, which then becomes "Right View"; insight leads to wisdom which cuts off ignorance (Cantwell 2010b). Craving subsequently lessens, fulfilling the Buddhist goal of ending suffering.

In addition to discipline, Buddhism suggests two approaches: (1) *samatha* (Pāli) meditation for the practice of mental concentration (Pāli: *samādhi*) and (2) *vipassanā* (Pāli) meditation for wisdom (Pāli: *paññā*). Our mind is usually differentiated. *Samatha* means the unification and the one-pointed-ness of the mind (Pāli: *cittassa ekaggatā*) being part of the higher state of meditative experience (Pāli: *jhāna*). *Samatha* is, according to the *Buddha*, only a means to the end, the end being the realization of wisdom (Karunadasa 2015b). Externally, human beings are bombarded with a wide range of information and stimulation which are presented in the forms of vision, sound, smell, taste, touch, and ideas. In contact with the outside world, our mental faculties receive information and translate them into our internal consciousness of different perceptions of the sensations. To understand this world, we cannot think and act in the usual way, that is, a convoluted endless action and mental process, which keeps interacting and expanding. Buddhism suggests the meditative observation of a simple recurring phenomenon, for example, a simple flow of breath upon which we practice our ability to focus. Thinking without *samādhi* is like seeing through a glass of muddy water. Concentration is the process of acute focus and filtration, so still and calm that all the dust and pieces of impurities are settled to an extent that only clear, transparent water is left at the top. It is through *vipassanā* meditation that we achieve an accurate and clear perception of phenomena, getting rid of the problems and illusions caused by seeing impermanence as permanence, suffering as happiness, and selflessness as self. There is no right answer without first framing and focusing on the right question.

To practice mental concentration, the *Buddha* taught in the *Ānāpānasati Sutta* (MLDB. MN 118) that we should practice not by focusing on the external world, but looking inward to our breathing. We could follow the meditation teaching in the *Cūḷasuññata Sutta* (MLDB. MN 121) on the release from fabrications and in the *Mahāsuññata Sutta* (MLDB. MN 122) on the release from our bodily movements, our mind agenda in speech and thought as well as the fabrication of self from the five aggregates. The *Anumāna Sutta* (MLDB. MN 5) suggests that conceit or ego are the most important and difficult qualities for monks to admonish. Grasping of our "self" would lead to contempt of others' views and attachment to our views to an extent that we would conceal our blemishes, as discussed in the *Anaṅgaṇa Sutta* (MLDB. MN 5). The "self" is therefore also described as the "mother of all blemishes". This fixation on self and self-view can be addressed through inferring whatever unwholesome qualities are in us as if they are in others. This is an effective way of practice because, this way, we are getting rid of the idea of "self" by equating our "self" to "others". On the other hand, if we only look outward by looking at the blemishes of others, we will never be able to reflect upon our blemishes and our self because the notion of "self" is further inflated and promoted by stepping on others' egos.

With mindfulness practice, we would then become "aware" of the conditionality of our acts and consciousness. Instead of letting our subconscious fabrications determine our ways of thinking in an autopilot mode, we are mindful of our thoughts and take them back to the path of liberation and happiness. Mindfulness is critical to happiness by guarding against "negative thoughts and wrongful practices" (Chang 2006). It would also allow us to train our mind to concentrate on a task, make the right decisions and thoughts, and be absorbed in calmness and equanimity—which is by itself a source of sustainable happiness (Fig. 11.1).

Fig. 11.1 Pay it forward. Note: Endless light lit by oil lamp on the path to Tigers Nest, Bhutan. (Source: Photo by author)

Virtues: Non-greed, Non-hatred, Non-delusion

Although observing the precepts is an integral part of moral practice, Buddhist teachings also place great importance on the cultivation of good qualities known as "virtues". In fact, each precept has a positive counterpart, respectively: (1) kindness and compassion to all living beings; (2) generosity and renunciation; (3) joyous satisfaction with one's own wife, contentment, and fewness-of-wishes; (4) loving truth by searching it out, recognizing falsity, and attaining precision of thought; and (5) mindfulness and clear awareness (Harvey 2013). Observances of the precepts are to become so intertwined with the personality of the individual that virtuous actions become second nature (Prebish and Keown 2006). Attaining such natural and spontaneous goodness is the goal of Buddhist ethics so that the most basic Buddhist "cardinal virtues", being non-greed (Pāli: *alobha*), non-hatred (Pāli: adosa), and non-delusion (Pāli: *amoha*), are just the opposite of the three "roots of evil" (Pāli: *akusala-mūla*) or "three poisons", namely, greed, hatred, and delusion.

With respect to the *Mahāyāna* (Skt.) tradition later developed in Buddhism, the Six Perfections (Pāli: *pārāmita*) provides a convenient tabulation of the virtues of a *Bodhisatta*, namely, generosity (Pāli: *dāna*), morality (Pāli: *sīla*), patience (Pāli: *khanti*), perseverance (Pāli: *viriya*), meditation (Pāli: *samādhi*), and wisdom (Pāli: *paññā*). Other virtues worth noting are *ahiṃsā* (Pāli), the virtue of non-violence or non-harming; and compassion (Pāli: *karuṇā*), which is highly valued in all schools of Buddhism, particularly by the *Mahāyāna* (Skt.) (Prebish and Keown 2006).

Frank's (1996) research confirmed the view that many people are capable of making economic choices concerning unselfish motives. People's sense of morality is positively correlated with higher job satisfaction. For example, some people feel less satisfied when their work colleagues engage in unethical behavior. They are also willing to sacrifice their annual compensation (or pay a premium) for socially responsible employers and occupations, which are considered to be socially responsible or serving a social mission. Despite the higher cost associated with their positive initiatives, research by Frank (2010) demonstrates that responsible organizations are rewarded by (1) reducing opportunistic behaviors between owners and managers, (2) solving commitment problems associated with customers or other firms, (3) building stronger customer loyalty, (4) lowering labor cost as employees may be willing to receive lower compensation to reflect a premium for moral satisfaction, (5) being more attractive to new recruits.

On the other hand, research also demonstrated that high self-control is generally beneficial and adaptive to a wide range of behaviors particularly in forming and breaking habits (De Ridder et al. 2012). Discipline is also built upon a sense of integrity and honesty to reflect and reveal successes and failures to oneself and others. Sustainable decision-makers are constantly in deep self-reflection. Over the last few decades, a high level of honesty and integrity has been consistently proven to be critical in crises. Poor managers in various frauds in these crises were exposed for not only withholding information from the public but intentionally manipulating facts to conceal their failures.

Compassion for Others: The *Buddha* and *Bodhisatta* Ideals

Mahāyāna (Skt.) Buddhism comprises a set of ideals, precepts, and practices which has their roots in early Buddhism regarding harmful and virtuous acts. Loving kindness (Pāli: *mettā*) and compassion (Pāli: *karuṇā*) are seen as part of the factor of "right resolve", which could deepen virtue and alleviate the attachment to "self". Together with altruistic joy (Pāli: *muditā*) and equanimity (Pāli: *upekkhā*), they are the four divine abodes (Pāli: *brahmavihāra*) taught by the *Buddha* which a practitioner should practice and dwell on. As discussed in the *Karaṇīyametta Sutta* (NDB. AN 4.125, AN 4.126), these four qualities can make the mind "immeasurable" and akin to the mind of the noble ones.

When ill will arises against someone, a person developing loving kindness should consider that a poisoned mind may cause more harm than the actions of an enemy. Getting angry is actually the same as causing oneself suffering (Harvey 2013). Practice of these four—loving kindness, compassion, sympathetic joy, and equanimity—will lead to a divine birth (Cantwell 2010b).

The first of the *Bodhisatta* transcendent actions, giving or generosity, is an important practice in Buddhism, "considered to create much virtue and long-term merit which can be taken from one life to the next"

(Cantwell 2010a). Within the Three Trainings, which are equally applicable to the *Bodhisatta*-s' practice, moral discipline (Pāli: *sīla*) encompasses the first aspect of generosity (Pāli: *dāna*) and the third of patience (Pāli: *khanti*) (Cantwell 2010a). It is linked to the Buddhist precepts with the aim of refraining from unwholesome or evil actions.

What makes *Mahāyāna* (Skt.) Buddhism distinctive from early Buddhism is the emphasis on compassion for others through a deep understanding of selflessness and emptiness. Instead of focusing on self-restraint for one's own spiritual progress toward the cessation of suffering, all virtues accumulated is dedicated to the enlightenment of all. In Eastern and Northern Buddhism traditions, the taking of the *Bodhisatta* vows is typically done after taking the Five Precepts and involves a solemn commitment to aid all beings. This is to be done by regular practice of the six "perfections" (*pārami*): generosity, virtue, patience, vigor, meditation, and wisdom. In Southern Buddhism tradition, there are ten perfections: generosity, virtue, non-sensuality, wisdom, vigor, patience, truthfulness, determination, loving kindness, and equanimity. Although a *Bodhisatta* develops these to the highest degree, they are recommended for all aiming for *nibbāna* (Harvey 2013).

While the Five Precepts or the Five Mindfulness Trainings above may focus more on personal development, the Fourteen Mindfulness Trainings (Thich 2012) is a modern adaptation of the *Bodhisatta* vows which focuses on the cultivation of concentration and insight to see that our happiness is not separate from the happiness of others. It is the modernized version of Buddhist training for *Bodhisatta*-s and the core training required to see inter-being and sustainability. The Fourteen Mindfulness Trainings are respectively (1) openness—awareness of the suffering created by fanaticism and intolerance; (2) non-attachment to views—awareness of the suffering created by attachment to views and wrong perceptions; (3) freedom of thought—awareness of the suffering brought about when we impose our views on others; (4) awareness of suffering—awareness that looking deeply at our own suffering can help us cultivate understanding and compassion; (5) compassionate, healthy living—awareness that happiness is rooted in peace, solidity, freedom, and compassion; (6) taking care of anger—awareness that anger blocks communication and creates suffering; (7) dwelling happily in the present moment—awareness that life is available only in the present moment; (8) true community and communication—awareness that lack of communication always brings separation and suffering; (9) truthful and loving speech—awareness that words can create happiness or suffering; (10) protecting and nourishing the *saṅgha*—awareness that the essence and aim of the *saṅgha* is the practice of understanding and compassion; (11) right livelihood—awareness that great violence and injustice have been done to our environment and society; (12) reverence for life—awareness that much suffering is caused by war and conflict; (13) generosity—awareness of the suffering caused by exploitation, social injustice, stealing, and oppression; and (14) right conduct—awareness that sexual desire is not love and that sexual relations motivated by craving cannot dissipate the feeling of loneliness.

When it comes to salvaging all sentient beings from all kinds of sufferings, the *Buddha* and *Bodhisatta* are particularly well-regarded in the *Mahāyāna* (Skt.) traditions for their compassion, wisdom, and transcendent power. In the *Lotus Sūtra*, the practice of the *Bodhisattva Avalokiteśvara* (Skt.) is acclaimed by the *Buddha* as the "Universal Gateway" because "[i]n all the worlds of the ten directions, there is no place where [the *Bodhisattva Avalokiteśvara*] will not manifest himself" (Kubo and Yuyama 2007). People in the midst of sufferings and calamities only have to contemplate his name and power; and the *Bodhisattva Avalokiteśvara* "will immediate perceive their voices and free them from their suffering". The *Bodhisattva Avalokiteśvara* "wanders through many lands in various forms, and saves sentient beings … [He] bestows fearlessness in times of fearful calamity". This is achievable because the *Bodhisattva Avalokiteśvara* has fully mastered wisdom and skillful means, and is free from all the wrong views, delusion, and attachment of the untrained mind. He perceives the world with truth, purity, and vast knowledge on the one hand, and benevolence and compassion on the other hand. The *Buddha* also teaches in the *Heart Sūtra* that because "there are no more obstacles in [the *Bodhisattva*-s' (Skt.)] mind, they can overcome all fear, destroy all wrong perceptions and realize Perfect Nirvana" (Thich 2014).

Box 11.2 Four Divine Abodes (*Brahmavihāra*)

In the *Loving-Kindness Sutta* (NDB. AN 4.125, AN 4.126), the *Buddha* taught that a practitioner should practice and dwell in the four divine abodes (Pāli: *brahmavihāra*), the abodes being loving kindness (Pāli: *mettā*), compassion (Pāli: *karuṇā*), altruistic joy (Pāli: *muditā*), and equanimity (Pāli: *upekkhā*).

Loving kindness is the hope that we will all be well and happy.

Compassion is the hope that we will all be free from suffering.

Altruistic joy is to rejoice in all of our happiness and virtues.

Equanimity is the freedom from duality.

For a disciple who "relishes, desires, finds satisfaction in" these four divine abodes with "equanimity, vast, exalted, measureless, without enmity, without ill will" (NDB. AN 4.125, AN 4.126), he would eventually be reborn in the company of *brahmā*, devas of streaming radiance, refulgent glory, and great fruit, respectively. He would eventually attain final *nibbāna* (NDB. AN 4.125, AN 4.126).

Hence, the *Buddha* taught that the achieved practitioner "contemplates whatever phenomena ... as impermanent, as suffering, as a disease, as a boil, as a dart, as misery, as an affliction, as alien, as disintegrating, as empty, as non-self" (NDB. AN 4.125, AN 4.126). Buddhist teachings could hence be loving and kind, compassionate, rejoicing, and truly impartial, seeking a practice of win-win for all in selflessness.

Chapter Summary

- The Threefold Trainings of moral discipline, metal concentration, and wisdom are in fact three stages of moral development corresponding to the three levels of expression of unskillful moral qualities.
- The practice of a moral life is a graduated discipline, a graduated course of conduct, and a graduated mode of progress of our mind and bodily actions.
- Moral disciplines ensure harmony in the mental and bodily actions within oneself, but also within a community, and should be enacted based on an empirical understanding of human minds and actions and how they affect development.

- The Five Precepts (Pāli: *pañca-sīla*):—not taking life, not taking what is not given, no sexual misconducts, no lying, no intoxicants—serve as the basis of Buddhist moral practice.
- Buddhism does not encourage strong guilt even if we fail to observe the precept. For an action to break a precept and be karmically harmful, it must be performed with intention.
- Responsible decision-makers should similarly integrate moral discipline, mental concentration, and wisdom into the decision-making process.
- To achieve sustainable happiness, decision-making must also abide by moral discipline. Happiness is possible only when our livelihood is consistent with morality and values, so that we do not cause harm or unhappiness to ourselves and others.
- Buddhism suggests two approaches: (1) *samādhi* (Pāli) meditation for the practice of mental concentration (Pāli: *samādhi*) and (2) *vipassanā* (Pāli) or insight meditation for wisdom (Pāli: *paññā*).
- Our mind is usually differentiated. *Samatha* (Pāli) means the unification and the one-pointed-ness of the mind (Pāli: *cittassa ekaggatā*) being part of the higher state of meditative experience (Pāli: *jhāna*). *Samatha* is, according to the *Buddha*, only a means to the end, the end being the realization of wisdom.
- With mindfulness practice, we would then become "aware" of the conditionality of our acts and consciousness. Instead of letting our subconscious fabrications determine our ways of thinking in an autopilot mode, we are mindful of our thoughts and take them back to the path of liberation and happiness.
- Although observing the precepts is an integral part of moral practice, Buddhist teachings also place great importance on the cultivation of good qualities known as "virtues".
- Research confirmed the view that many people are capable of making economic choices concerning unselfish motives. People's sense of morality is positively correlated with higher job satisfaction.
- Research also demonstrated that high self-control is generally beneficial and adaptive to a wide range of behaviors particularly in forming and breaking habits.
- *Mahāyāna* (Skt.) Buddhism comprises a set of ideals, precepts, and practices which has their roots in early Buddhism regarding harmful and virtuous acts.

- What makes *Mahāyāna* (Skt.) Buddhism distinctive from early Buddhism is the emphasis on compassion for others through a deep understanding of selflessness and emptiness. Instead of focusing on self-restraint for one's own spiritual progress toward the cessation of suffering, all virtues accumulated is dedicated to the enlightenment of all.
- When it comes to salvaging all sentient beings from all kinds of sufferings, the *Buddha* and *Bodhisatta* are particularly well-regarded in the *Mahāyāna* (Skt.) traditions for his compassion, wisdom, and transcendent power.
- The *Buddha* taught that a practitioner should practice and dwell in the four divine abodes (Pāli: *brahmavihāra*), the abodes being loving kindness (Pāli: *mettā*), compassion (Pāli: *karuṇā*), altruistic joy (Pāli: *muditā*), and equanimity (Pāli: *upekkhā*).

Study Questions

- Are the Five Precepts rules or restrictions that inhibit freedom?
- Is Buddhist moral theory also a dogmatic adherence to views?
- How is the observance of precepts related to responsible decision-making?
- Are compassion and wisdom instruments or strategies for better economic activities?
- Why are the four immeasurables also known as the four divine abodes?

Suggested Essay Topics

- Threefold Trainings and sustainable decision-making
- Five Precepts and Five Mindfulness Training in daily life
- *Bodhisatta* vows and the Fourteen Mindfulness Trainings
- Self-control and responsible decision-making
- Compassion and wisdom in daily life
- *Buddha* and *Bodhisatta* as role models of compassion and wisdom
- Compassion and wisdom in the market economy

Bibliography

Online Multimedia

Singer, Peter. 2013. *The Why and How of Effective Altruism*. TED. Accessed 28 Aug 2019. https://www.ted.com/talks/peter_singer_the_why_and_how_of_effective_altruism/up-next#t-5416

Required Reading

Harvey, Peter. 2013. Buddhist Practices: Ethics. In *An Introduction to Buddhism: Teachings, History and Practices*, 2nd ed., 268–282. New York: Cambridge University Press. Original edition, 1990.

Further Reading

Bodhi, Bhikkhu. 2012. *The Numerical Discourses of the Buddha: A Translation of the Aṅguttara Nikāya*. Translated by from the *Pāli* by Bhikkhu Bodhi. Somerville: Wisdom Publications.

Cantwell, Cathy. 2010a. The Three Trainings: I Moral Discipline. In *Buddhism: The Basics*, 69–79. London/New York: Routledge.

———. 2010b. The Three Trainings: II Meditative Absorption. In *Buddhism: The Basics*, 79–83. London/New York: Routledge.

Chang, Otto H. 2006. Buddhist Approach to Economic Development: The Path to A Wisdom-based Economy. *The Hsi Lai Journal of Humanistic Buddhism* 7: 173–181.

De Ridder, Denise T.D., Gerty Lensvelt-Mulders, Catrin Finkenauer, F. Marijn Stok, and Roy F. Baumeister. 2012. Taking Stock of Self-Control: A Meta-Analysis of How Trait Self-Control Relates to a Wide Range of Behaviors. *Personality and Social Psychology Review* 16 (1): 76–99.

Frank, Robert H. 1996. What Price the Moral High Ground? *Southern Economic Journal* 63 (1): 1–17.

———. 2010. *What Price the Moral High Ground?: Ethical Dilemmas in Competitive Environments*. Princeton: Princeton University Press. Original edition, 2004.

Karunadasa, Yakupitiyage. 2001. *The Early Buddhist Teaching on the Practice of the Moral Life*. The Numata Yehan Lecture in Buddhism Fall 2001, University of Calgary.

———. 2015a. *Early Buddhist Teachings: The Middle Position in Theory and Practice*. Hong Kong: Centre of Buddhist Studies, The University of Hong Kong.

———. 2015b. The Role of Meditation in the Threefold Scheme of Buddhist Mental Culture. In *Buddhist Meditative Praxis: Traditional Teachings & Modern Applications*, ed. K.L. Dhammajoti, 117–122. Hong Kong: Centre of Buddhist Studies, The University of Hong Kong.

Kubo, Tsugunari, and Arika Yuyama, trans. 2007. The Gateway to Every Direction [Manifested by Bodhisattva Avalokiteśvara]. In *The Lotus Sūtra* (Translated from the Chinese of *Taishō* Volume 9, Number 262 of Kumārajiva), 2nd ed., 301. Berkeley: Numata Center for Buddhist Translation and Research.

MLDB. MN 118. Ānāpānasati Sutta: Mindfulness of Breathing. In *MLDB*, 941–949. Somerville: Wisdom Publications.

MLDB. MN 121. Cūḷasuññatasutta: The Shorter Discourse on Voidness. In *MLDB*, 965–970. Somerville: Wisdom Publications.

MLDB. MN 5. Anaṅgaṇa Sutta: Without Blemishes. In *MLDB*, 108–114. Somerville: Wisdom Publications.

MLDB. MN 61. Ambalaṭṭhikārāhulovāda Sutta: Advice to Rahula at Ambalatthika. In *MLDB*. Somerville: Wisdom Publications.

Ñanamoli, Bhikkhu, and Bhikkhu Bodhi. 1995. *The Middle Length Discourses of the Buddha: A Translation of the Majjhima Nikaya (Teachings of the Buddha)*. Somerville: Wisdom Publications.

NDB. AN 10.51. One's Own Mind. In *NDB*, 1402–1403. Somerville: Wisdom Publications.

NDB. AN 4.125, AN 4.126. Loving-Kindness (1) & (2). In *NDB*, 507–510. Somerville: Wisdom Publications.

NDB. AN 5.177. Trades. In *NDB*, 790. Somerville: Wisdom Publications.

NDB. AN 8.39. Streams. In *NDB*, 1173–1175. Somerville: Wisdom Publications.

Ng, Ernest C.H. 2018. Mindfulness and Buddhist Economics in the Financial Market–Generating Delta or Alpha? *Society and Economy* 40 (4): 515–529.

Prebish, Charles S., and Damien Keown. 2006. Ethics. In *Buddhism-The Ebook*, 333–347. Journal of Buddhist Ethics Online Books.

Thich, Nhat Hanh. 2009. The Five Mindfulness Trainings. Accessed 1 Dec 2015. http://plumvillage.org/mindfulness-practice/the-5-mindfulness-trainings/

———. 2012. *The Fourteen Mindfulness Trainings*. Accessed 1 Dec 2015. http://plumvillage.org/mindfulness-practice/the-14-mindfulness-training

———, trans. 2014. *The Insight that Brings Us to the Other Shore*. Translated from *The Heart Sūtra*. Accessed 2 Aug 2016. http://plumvillage.org/wp-content/uploads/2014/09/2014-Thich-Nhat-Hanh-New-Heart-Sutra-letter-cc.pdf

CHAPTER 12

Implications for Business, and for Social and Environmental Change

Buddhist Perspective on Effecting Sustainable Change

The Buddhist doctrine of dependent arising and impermanence posits that change is a fundamental part of realities. Our bodies, our thoughts, the events and objects we encounter and experience, all are subject to change. Understanding and managing favorable sustainable change is important to our personal, financial, and social well-being. Changes are imposed upon us involuntarily, while in other circumstances humans introduce changes proactively to further enhance the favorable conditions or alleviate adverse conditions. The silver lining of impermanence, perhaps, is that no unpleasant, dissatisfactory, or "bad-luck" experience will last forever.

Karunadasa (2015) explained the nature of impermanence thus: "Only when there is change, there is possibility of changeability." In Buddhist teachings, the human personality is "something plastic and pliable and therefore wieldable and amenable to change", hence the possibility to "descend" or "transcend". The *Buddha* said that even if a portion as small as a pinch of dust defies change in the psychophysical personality of a human being, then practicing the higher life is of no avail. Similarly, the state of our mental health, just like our physical health, is not permanent; it can be affected by major life events and trivial incidents alike. In the face of life's challenges, we have a choice: to cultivate the serenity to accept our circumstances, to find the courage to change our circumstances, and to

E. C. H. Ng, *Introduction to Buddhist Economics*,
Studies in Buddhist Economics, Management, and Policy,
https://doi.org/10.1007/978-3-030-35114-4_12

cultivate the wisdom to know what can or cannot be changed.[1] From the Buddhist perspective, serenity, courage, and wisdom can be cultivated within each of us, and through practice we can become more serene, courageous, and wise in the change-management process.

This process of sustainable change management applies to all relationship among individuals, organizations, societies, and the entire ecosystem. Sheng Yen (2019) proposed that in dealing with any difficulty in life, we can attempt to address it by the four steps: face it, accept it, deal with it, and then let it go. The key wisdom is to appreciate the Middle Way between what we can and what we cannot do with ourselves, others in the organizations, societies, and the entire ecosystem. What we can do is to face these challenges intellectually, physically, and psychologically. There are always people, subjects, and circumstances we like and dislike, yet we need to embrace them and deal with them. We can make an effort to be part of the change process, patiently and relentlessly, but we must also understand that immediate desirable goals may not be achievable here and now. We must appreciate that meaningful and sustainable change requires many favorable conditions over a long period to materialize.

On the contrary, failing to understand and manage the various constituents in this complex change process will lead to conflict, violence, and even wars. As Thich (2010) reiterates:

> The other person has wrong perceptions about himself and about us. And we have wrong perceptions about ourselves and the other person. And that is the foundation for violence and conflict and war … Both sides are motivated by fear, by anger, and by wrong perceptions.

However, the fear, anger, and wrong perceptions could not be resolved by confrontations, violence, or weapons. They should be removed by deep listening, compassionate listening, and loving speech. It is impossible to develop the right understanding and right perspective on ourselves and others without good communication in the form of loving speech and deep listening; it is impossible to cultivate loving speech and deep listening without moral values as the foundation: for if there is no trust, there is no basis for mutual understanding. It is with moral values that we can develop

[1]Adapted from the Serenity Prayer by American theologian Reinhold Niebuhr (1892–1971): "God, grant me the serenity to accept the things I cannot change, courage to change the things I can, and wisdom to know the difference."

the foundation of communication, cultivate the compassion and wisdom necessary to build mutual understanding, develop the wisdom to appreciate each other's circumstances.

While the change-makers may be frustrated by the entrenched and rigid thoughts and the established institutions of vested interests and bureaucracies, incumbents may also be disappointed by change-makers for their lack of appreciation of the complex and historical context of the change process. These conflicts of thought and generation seem to be a conflict of serenity and courage, but they may also represent a divide in wisdom—in understanding each other's perspective, in appreciating the dependent arising nature of all phenomena, and in appreciating how, together, we can be the change we wish to see. It is a transformation from self-centeredness to selflessness. With the Buddhist doctrine of dependent arising, we should abandon the *silo* mentality and see others' problems as our problems, embrace their challenges as our challenges. We should realize that we are the environment and we are the market. We mistakenly adopt the view that others' happiness has no bearing on our own happiness, or others' suffering has no influence on our own suffering. If we can truly appreciate our interdependence, we should be able to see that the well-being of each of us is neither the same nor independent. We are different but we are also interconnected. We are responsible for our own individual happiness as well as that of the community. Most importantly, we may begin to appreciate that both sides of any conflict are interdependent—we are together on the same ship. If there is no interdependence, there is no basis for either conflict or harmony.

The path of peace and reconciliation is never an easy one. It takes persistence, perseverance, compassion, and wisdom. Welford (2007) proclaims that Buddhist Economics could be a "peaceful individually based revolution." We could all initiate change from within each of us individually, now, without the need to wait or confront with institutions or other incumbents through radical changes.

Buddhist Economics in Business and Society

Buddhist teachings could inspire sustainable change and management practices in business and society because there is no corporation in history that can compete with the long-lasting influence of the *Buddha*—with an admirable global presence and network on every continent. The teachings, vision, and mission of the *Buddha* have been passed on from generation to generation. Many practitioners (successors of the *Buddha*) have had to overcome unbearable hardships and challenges to continue this legacy, especially when they venture out into new grounds. The Buddhist teachings attempt to adapt themselves to local circumstances and lifestyles, without losing sight of the core principles and values. It offers a very inspiring localized and customized solution by which the *Buddha*'s legacy is adjusted to meet human needs.

To improve and sustain competitiveness over time and space, modern enterprises focus on business models and standardization. They want to generate and maintain a good relationship with all stakeholders: customers, partners, investors, the management team, and staff members. Like all other kinds of relationships, we want to sustain these relationships through good times and bad. The *Buddha*'s approach, however, does not start from some grand design or plan. The "certification" or "endorsement" of the Buddhist teachings does not require complex ISO or Six Sigma standardization. After all, Buddhist practices aim to purify our minds, and all those superficial measurements are incapable of fathoming the depth and rigor of a practitioner's mind—one's mind is beyond measurement and beyond assessment by an outsider. Just as a proof by a world-class mathematician is indecipherable to a layperson, how could an exchange between two Buddhist masters be easily comprehended? For thousands of years of human history, the most sophisticated transmission of knowledge has taken place in the forms of value and spirituality: culture, philosophy, religion, a family legacy, and so forth. And one of the most effective models of sustainable transmission of ideas and knowledge through mentorship, coaching, and apprenticeship.

Moral discipline should revive its important role in business and societal decision-making, even in a competitive and profit-seeking economy. Using the finance sector as an example, Langevoort (2014) suggests that professions could adopt a right livelihood approach in identifying the right job by assessing (1) how much aggressiveness is required to be successful; (2) how success is defined; and (3) whether ethics plays an explicit role in the compliance function. He recommends the importance of perspective and reflection in thinking about our identity and actions through the eyes of others and seeing clients as our mother or someone we care about. To foster and nurture this commitment to ethical behavior, a mentor and ethical reminders should be identified. On the other hand, Dalio (2011) emphasizes the significance of radical transparency in achieving meaningful work and meaningful relationships. He believes that it is important to be honest with oneself and others so that communication could contribute to understanding the truth necessary for decision-making and self-improvement. It is through this level of transparency and integrity that people can engage in meaningful work and build meaningful relationships. Dalio is not afraid of making mistakes, as long as he could identify, analyze, and learn from them. It is important to develop "good habits of ethical awareness and ethical reflection that don't get caught up in self-serving rationalization" (Langevoort 2014).

With respect to mental concentration, research by Lo et al. (2005) demonstrated the relationship between investment trading performance and emotional reaction of financial traders. They argue that the ability to perform in investment decision-making does not necessarily relate to innate personality profiles—there is no specific "trader personality type". Good investors could be developed, trained, and practiced as a skill. Instead there seems to be a strong link between "emotional reactivity and trading performance" in financial decision-making, specifically in this case the intensity of reaction to "monetary gains and losses". Their results suggest that "extreme emotional response[s] are apparently counterproductive" and hence a potential means to develop a successful investment decision is to develop a reduced level of emotional reactions. Instead of allowing automatic emotional responses such as fear and greed (mediated by the amygdala) to dominate, they recommended that one could allow for more controlled or higher-level responses (mediated by the prefrontal cortex) to guide decision-making.

Recent interviews and reports have offered valuable feedback from successful decision-makers practicing mental concentration. The former chief investment officer of the Government of Singapore Investment Corporation, Ng Kok Song, commented that meditation could help investment professionals "by allowing one to emerge with a clear mind ... transcending our ego ... habitual mode of self-centeredness" (Rowe 2015) and "[g]reater clarity makes you more orderly" (Rathbone 2013). Dalio attributes his investment success to meditation. He believes that it is also very useful in generating creative thought, and in evaluating and responding to the overload of information in the market (Saft 2013). He said that meditation "gives me a centeredness, it gives me an ability to look at things without the emotional hijacking, without the ego, in a way that gives me a certain clarity" (Saft 2013). When he meditates, he said, "I acquire an equanimity that allows me to see things from a higher-level perspective and that allows me to make sensible decisions" (Rathbone

2013). Bill Gross, the founder of the world's largest fixed income fund PIMCO, suggests that meditation helps him remove "confirmation bias" (Rathbone 2013). Philipp Hildebrand, the vice-chairman of BlackRock and the former head of the Swiss National Bank, suggested that the time spent on meditation is "a pause that refreshes" (Rathbone 2013). Hafenbrack et al. (2014) provided data in support of mindfulness meditation as it positively correlates with increased resistance to the sunk-cost bias, even with a 15-minute mindfulness-meditation induction. People have sunk-cost biases when they fail to delineate present decision-making from the choices they made in the past, because of either the cost or the effort incurred. Through meditation, resistance to this sunk-cost bias increases by developing a temporal focus on the present, instead of wandering between the present, past, and future, and reducing negative regretful feelings that hinder the rational decision-making process.[2]

Business organizations have also been adopting awareness and compassion as important management values. One of the thought leaders in this area is Fred Kofman, a vice-president at LinkedIn. His initiative in conscious business illustrates how it can allow us to find our passion and express our essential values through our work. He argues that "a conscious business seeks to promote the intelligent pursuit of happiness in all its stakeholders ... [It produces] sustainable, exceptional performance through the solidarity of its community and the dignity of each member" (Kofman 2006). A new field of research in "compassion organization" also proves that when organizations promote the value of compassion rather than stress, they can contribute both a happier workplace and an improved bottom line. One of the reasons behind the improved well-being of employees in a compassionate organization is that compassion strengthens social connection. Recent developments of GNH in Business (NG 2018a) and Corporate Consciousness (Barrett 2013) are important efforts to embrace a more holistic set of parameters to measure performance and success of an organization. Business leaders should realize that success means making not only themselves but others rich. With a deep sense of contentment and shared fortune with the less fortunate ones, they could realize how their benevolent acts could make an impact on others' well-being, without necessarily affecting their own well-being. In his philanthropy pledge, Buffett fully appreciates that "time", "health", and

[2] See Ng (2018b) for further discussion on Mindfulness and Buddhist Economics in financial market decision-making.

"interesting, diverse, and long-standing friends" are much more valuable than money. Spending an extra one percent on himself would not contribute to his own happiness or his well-being. But it would have a significant impact on the health and welfare of others (Acs 2013).

Buddhist Economics and Environmental Protection

Instead of seeing nature as an integral part of our life and source of inspiration, modern economy has narrowed it simply as resources to be controlled and deployed in exchange for progress. The root of the "ecocrisis"—pollution, resource depletion, erosion, deforestation—is built upon some fallacious illusions that human happiness and well-being lie in the satisfaction of material needs and sensual desires at the expense of nature (Bodhi 1987). As investigated in previous chapters, Buddhism has a significant world-view on the notion of needs, desires, and happiness. The core tenet of Buddhist teachings is that all sentient beings like happiness and dislike pain, even though their desires and sensitivities may vary (Harvey 2000). Hence the *Karaṇīyametta Sutta* speaks of radiating loving kindness to all types of beings. Fundamentally, as opposed to seeing nature (animals, plants, and the physical environment) as only neighbors, resources, or even enemies, Thich (1988) reminds us of the Buddhist teachings of interbeing: "we should deal with nature the way we should deal with ourselves! We should not harm ourselves; we should not harm nature ... Human beings and nature are inseparable" (Fig. 12.1).

This inseparable understanding of interbeing is depicted in the *Avataṃsaka Sūtra* (Skt.) as the "Jewel Net of Indra" where each thing in this web is "interpenetrated" by every other, contributing to and supporting each other and the whole. The *Sūtra* says, "every living being and every minute thing is significant, since even the tiniest thing contains the whole mystery" (Harvey 2000). It is a deep interrelationship of all things, so we must respect other beings and the environment we depend on, and be aware of how our negative actions toward the rest of nature go on to affect us. We influence the environment through not only physical actions, but also the attached moral or immoral qualities (Harvey 2000). As illustrated in the *Aggañña-sutta*, mankind and the natural world evolved together (Prebish and Keown 2006). We depend on nature for resources, particularly those living a rural life. It is therefore our "moral duty to protect and foster it with gratitude like part of a family" (Harvey 2000).

Fig. 12.1 The bell of wisdom and peace. Note: The bell of wisdom and peace at the Root Temple (*Tu Hieu*) of the Plum Village, Hue, Vietnam. (Source: Photo by author)

Even though humans are born with greater capacity and potential in moral and spiritual developments than other animals, Buddhist teachings do not sanction human beings a natural-born superiority, dominance, or stewardship (Harvey 2000). Instead of a hierarchy of sentient beings, more appropriate division should be that between sentient beings and the non-sentient environment—sentience as "the ability to experience and to suffer, and the related ability, in this or a future life, to transcend suffering by attaining enlightenment" (Harvey 2000). Humans' superior capabilities should mean a higher level of moral responsibility—an ideal of *noblesse oblige* (Hall, 1902). Our relationship with animals, plants, and the landscape is one of harmonious cooperation but not domination. The *Buddha* specifically praised the Brahmins for not sacrificing animals for rituals—such sparing of animal lives is known as not killing in the Five Precepts or the "gift of fearlessness" (*abhayadāna*). In fact, the *Buddha*'s emphasis was on the avoidance of killing or violence against other animals, instead of avoidance of meat-eating. Vegetarianism is advocated particularly in a certain *Mahāyāna* (Skt.) tradition but it is not mandatory for all Buddhists. If sacrificing animals for rituals to higher beings is not praised, the use of animals in product testing, in medical research, and in training is unlikely to be defendable as sacrifices for human well-being.

Nature is also a source of inspiration, allowing practitioners to cultivate an intuitive appreciation of the subtle but intrinsic "suchness" which appears and operates in everything and everywhere (Harvey 2000). However, it cannot be easily recognized without letting go of one's ego and being absorbed into the vastness of nature. Even the *Buddha*'s own spiritual journey was surrounded by nature, from birth, enlightenment, first sermon to nirvana. Nevertheless, he was not only attached to nature and he taught from town to town, city to city.

Deep Ecology

While humans' relationship with the environment has been analyzed from a scientific perspective, Naess (1973) argues that it is important to go beyond the limit of science and explore the philosophical aspect of ecological harmony based on each of our own belief systems. This individual ecosophy—eco philosophy—together with the potential change, is part of the two core directions of Deep Ecology. The Deep Ecology approach was not invented by Naess. The search for higher wisdom beyond the technical aspect of science has long since been an integral part of human history. The approach answers not only "how to live" but ethical questions on "how we should live" (Ims 2015). Deep Ecology assumes a "relational … total field perspective, and it focuses on the underlying causes; the roots of the problems"—including deep reflection and change on the idea of man as a subject. Like Buddhist teachings, Deep Ecology is a holistic worldview which connects humans with the rest of nature. Naess (1989) claims that the fate of humanity and nature is intertwined: we are hurting ourselves if we hurt nature. What is required is therefore a long-term, deeper cure as opposed to the shallow ecology which is a "technocratic attitude" of addressing the symptoms through technological fixes—whether it be regulations, technologies, levies, and so forth. The shallow approach implies that progress and affluence are vital and hence other sacrifices are necessary to keep the consumption and production levels intact (Ims 2015).

Deep Ecology is both "a philosophical approach and a campaigning platform. It is a process of reflection leading to action" (Ims 2015). It encourages people from different professions to work together in contributing different perspective and expertise. It would involve a good fusion of *unity* and *diversity*, meaning working together without losing differences in perspectives (Ims 2015). It is a framework with four levels of questioning and articulation going back and forth to keep our higher-level beliefs in sync with practical actions. While it advocates equal value between human and other sentient beings, it also acknowledges the enormous power and responsibility human beings have in the system. According to Ims (2015), it can therefore be "simple in means and rich in ends". The importance of considering ecosophy as a "personal position—a personal total world-view"—is that it is totally actionable for everyone at a day-to-day level. It demands each one of us to make a difference by provoking changes in the system by our respective capabilities. Together, economy as the rational materialistic consideration, ecosophy as the spiritual philosophical framework, and ecology form a new trinity that could potentially rebalance the existing relationship between humans and the environment.

Envisioning a Sustainable Transformation

Fully establishing the relationship between Buddhist values and economic development is difficult not only because of the challenges in quantifying the degree of Buddhist influence—the impact of Buddhist teachings on the decision-making process of individuals, corporates, and society as a whole—but also in tracing the links, both possible and casual, between Buddhism and economic change. As evident by the strong regional variations of economic growth across the world, differences in local culture can have a strong influence on the economy. And religion has an important role in shaping the social structures, value systems, and institutions supporting the economic systems. The impact of values on economic behavior should be fully analyzed in conjunction with understanding sustainable economic development, because different belief systems will have a significant but often underrated influence on the factors driving economic decision-makings. From a religious and spiritual perspective, it is inadequate to oversimplify complex human desires, motives, and welfare by assuming all human beings are the same rational economic man across different spheres (Daniels 1998).

Daniels (1998) conducted a unique study to evaluate the relationship between Buddhist influence with various factors relating to economic development. To some extent, Buddhist otherworldly orientation may appear to be unconducive to diligence and secular achievement and Buddhism does consider material attachment the cause of adverse human conditions. Early theories, particularly in Weber's work, suggest that Eastern philosophy and religion were not supportive of capitalism and economic growth, particularly with its focus on spirituality and values over rationality. However, Buddhist values such as "devotion, discipline, concentration, sobriety, tolerance and sacrifice" are supportive of economic activity. The teaching of "right livelihood" is quite consistent with the initiatives on Environmental, Social and Governance (ESG) issues. Two of the principal Buddhist *pāramitā* (Pāli), vigorous exertion and concentration (Alexandrin, 1981), are also supportive of economic development. According to Daniels (1998), other Buddhist doctrines that are compatible with modern scientific world-views are (1) focus on insight and knowledge, (2) cultivation of knowledge through critical investigation, personal experience, and verification, (3) emphasis on personal enlightenment building upon understanding the reality, (4) respect for education, (5) adherence to a causal approach in the conception of a universe, and so on. While self-interest and competition are regarded as the fundamental values of market economy, a selfish, hostile, and deceitful environment is undoubtedly detrimental to economic growth.

Daniels (1998) established that Buddhist teachings on reducing materialistic desire and a simpler lifestyle can alleviate pressure on the environment, but it may also reduce economies of scale and efficiency. The track record of countries with strong Buddhist influence ("BI nations") may not maintain the standard of social and political equality and justice we anticipate. BI nations might still report a high level of energy consumption and environmental exploitation. On the other hand, they have also reported a higher life expectancy, a higher literacy rate, and a lower population growth rate. Economic success is reported in countries where Buddhist influence may not be that high or with a stronger relationship with *Mahāyāna* (Skt.). Overall, it is not easy to identify "any consistent patterns and unique features of economic change for the BI nations".

Nevertheless, a sustainable transformation toward Buddhist Economics is possible by transforming our understanding of the notion of "I" through a six "I"s strategy. It is an attempt to implement the essence of Buddhist world-view and economic strategy. The first and second "I"s are the transformation from *individual* to *integral*. Self-interest and individual ideas were prioritized in the market economy but the true meaning of self-identity is misconceived. Our identity is falsely built on a false fabrication of self—manifested through consumption and work choices. Even though our consumption and work are reflective of our thoughts and decision-making philosophies, a homogenous permanent self does not exist.

Nonetheless, the decisions we made in the market economy do have profound consequences. The Buddhist teachings advise us to be mindful of how we consume and make a living; these choices interact with our consciousness. We are not robots and we should be able to deliver our best potential. Similarly, we should treat capital in coherence with our value proposition: how we generate and deploy it. As Emerson (2002) advocates, any foundation, trust, and organization should consider capital as a continuum. It is schizophrenic if an entity exploits child labor on the one hand and donates to protect children on the other. Even though we may have different roles from time to time, we should be able to act consistently, integrating our values and behaviors.

The third and fourth "I"s are the transformation from *independence* to *interdependence*. The practice of mindfulness allows us to develop insight to realize that our notion of self is inseparable from others in the community and the environment. We need to understand that we are interdependent with the market and the environment. For sustainable change, more time and patience is required to reconfigure the policies or structures not only on the surface, but also on the fundamental root causes and necessary conditions.

The fifth and sixth "I"s are the transformation from *ignorance* to *insight*. Insight comprises the information and wisdom to understand the karmic causes and consequences of our actions, as well as the profound meaning of interconnectedness and selflessness. It is also the wisdom required to deeply understand the significance of time, the patience required to change thoughts and behaviors, and the wisdom to know the difference between what can and cannot be changed in the short term. Finally, insight should also include a deep understanding of the enormous potential of human minds. When we are in delusion, our mind is driven by circumstances; when we are enlightened, our minds can change the circumstances.

Chapter Summary

- Karunadasa explained the nature of impermanence thus: "Only when there is change, there is possibility of changeability." In the Buddhist teachings, the human personality is "something plastic and pliable and therefore wieldable and amenable to change", hence the possibility to "descend" or "transcend".
- Meaningful and sustainable change requires many favorable conditions over a long period to materialize. Failing to understand and manage the various constituents in this complex change process will lead to conflict, violence, and even wars.
- Fear, anger, and wrong perceptions could not be resolved by confrontations, violence, or weapons. They should be removed by deep listening, compassionate listening, and loving space.
- All sentient beings like happiness and dislike pain, even though their desires and sensitivities may vary. Humans' superior capabilities should mean a higher level of moral responsibility—an ideal of *noblesse oblige*.
- Our relationship with animals, plants, and the landscape is one of harmonious cooperation but not domination. Thich Nhat Hanh reminds us of the Buddhist teachings of interbeing: "we should deal with nature the way we should deal with ourselves! ... Human beings and nature are inseparable."
- We depend on nature for resources, particularly those living a rural life. It is therefore our "moral duty to protect and foster it with gratitude like part of a family".
- Arne Naess argues that it is important to go beyond the limit of science and explore the philosophical aspect of ecological harmony based on each of our own belief systems.
- Ecosophy is not only "how to live" but "how we should live". Deep Ecology assumes a "relational ... total field perspective, and it focuses on the underlying causes; the roots of the problems".
- Impact of values on economic behavior should be fully analyzed in conjunction with understanding sustainable economic development; different belief systems will have a significant influence on the factors driving economic decision-makings.
- Fully assessing the relationship between Buddhism and economic change is difficult: the challenges are in quantifying the degree of Buddhist influence, and in tracing the links, both possible and casual.

- A sustainable transformation to Buddhist Economics is possible by transforming our understanding of the notion of "I" through a six "I"s strategy: from *individual* to *integral*; from *independence* to *interdependence*; from *ignorance* to *insight*.

Study Questions

- Is the doctrine of impermanence in contradiction with sustainability?
- How to impose sustainable changes?
- Why is it not possible to resolve conflicts by confrontations, violence, or weapons?
- Are humans superior to plants, animals, or the ecosystem?
- How is Deep Ecology different from ecology?
- Is it possible to demonstrate the relationship between Buddhist values and social changes?

Suggested Essay Topics

- Sustainability in the midst of impermanence
- Buddhist Economic strategy in implementing sustainable change
- Buddhist philosophies in conflict resolution
- Deep Ecology and Buddhist Economics
- Buddhist Economics and economic changes

Bibliography

Online Multimedia

Arthus-Bertrand, Yann. 2016. Terra – A Film by Yann Arthus-Bertrand. *Terra Omega*. Last modified 1 May 2016. https://www.youtube.com/watch?v=5pMScorWcyU

Emerson, Jed. 2019. Ethically Motivated Investing Rising Globally. *Deutsche Welle*. Last modified 30 Sept 2019. https://p.dw.com/p/3QULL

Required Reading

Harvey, Peter. 2000. Attitude to and Treatment of the Natural World. In *An Introduction to Buddhist Ethics: Foundations, Values and Issues*, 150–185. Cambridge: Cambridge University Press. Reprint, Seventh.

Ims, Knut J. 2015. Deep Ecology and Personal Responsibility. In *The Spiritual Dimension of Business Ethics and Sustainability Management*, ed. László Zsolnai, 47–56. Cham: Springer.

Further Reading

Acs, Zoltan J. 2013. *Why Philanthropy Matters: How the Wealthy Give, and What It Means for Our Economic Well-Being*. Princeton and Oxford: Princeton University Press.

Alexandrin, Glen. 1981. Buddhist Economics: An Economics of the Middle Way. *Ghandi Marg* 2 (11): 627–637.

Barrett, Richard. 2013. *Liberating the Corporate Soul—Building a Visionary Organization*. London and New York: Routledge.

Bodhi, Bhikkhu. 1987. Foreword. In *Buddhist Perspective on the Ecocrisis*, ed. Klas Sandell, 5–10. Kandy: BPS. The Wheel Publication No. 346–348.

Dalio, Ray. 2011. Principles. Accessed 1 Dec 2015. http://www.bwater.com/Uploads/FileManager/Principles/Bridgewater-Associates-Ray-Dalio-Principles.pdf

Daniels, Peter L. 1998. Economic Change, the Environment and Buddhism in Asia. *International Journal of Social Economics* 25 (6/7/8): 968–1004.

Emerson, Jed. 2002. *A Capital Idea: Total Foundation Asset Management and the Unified Investment Strategy*. Accessed 1 Dec 2015. https://www.gsb.stanford.edu/gsb-cmis/gsb-cmis-download-auth/318001

Hafenbrack, Andrew C., Zoe Kinias, and Sigal G. Barsade. 2014. Debiasing the Mind Through Meditation: Mindfulness and the Sunk-Cost Bias. *Psychological Science* 25 (2): 369–376.

Hall, Fielding. 1902. *The Soul of a People*. London: Macmillan.

Harvey, Peter. 2000. *An Introduction to Buddhist Ethics: Foundations, Values and Issues*. Cambridge: Cambridge University Press.

Karunadasa, Yakupitiyage. 2015. *Early Buddhist Teachings: The Middle Position in Theory and Practice*. Hong Kong: Centre of Buddhist Studies, The University of Hong Kong.

Kofman, Fred. 2006. *Conscious Business: How to Build Value through Values*. Boulder: Sounds True.

Langevoort, Donald C. 2014. *Ethical Mindfulness: A Guide for New Financial Services Professionals*. CFA Institute. Accessed 1 Dec 2015. https://www.cfainstitute.org/learning/future/Documents/Ethical%20Mindfulness.pdf

Lo, Andrew W., Dmitry V. Repin, and Brett N. Steenbarger. 2005. Cognitive Neuroscientific Foundations of Behavior: Fear and Greed in Financial Markets: A Clinical Study of Day-traders. *The American Economic Review* 95 (2): 352–359.

Naess, Arne. 1973. The Shallow and the Deep, Long-Range Ecology Movement. *Inquiry* 16: 95–100.

———. 1989. *Ecology, Community and Lifestyle*. Translated and edited by David Rothenberg. Cambridge: Cambridge University Press.

Ng, Ernest C.H. 2018a. Corporate Sustainability and Legacy Building in Business Through the GNH Framework. In *GNH of Business—Proceedings of the Seventh International Conference on Gross National Happiness*, ed. Dasho Karma Ura and Sangay Chophel, 369–392. Thimphu: The Centre of Bhutan Studies & GNH.

———. 2018b. Mindfulness and Buddhist Economics in the Financial Market–Generating Delta or Alpha? *Society and Economy* 40 (4): 515–529. https://doi.org/10.1556/204.2018.40.4.3.

Prebish, Charles S., and Damien Keown. 2006. Ecology. In *Buddhism-The Ebook*, 324–332. Journal of Buddhist Ethics Online Books. 2005.

Rathbone, John P. 2013. Zen and the Art of Managment. *Financial Times*, September 16. http://www.ft.com/intl/cms/s/2/32e0b9b4-1c5f-11e3-8894-00144feab7de.html#axzz3rvA9g1KJ

Rowe, Sam Del. 2015. The Importance of Meditation for Investment Professionals. CFA Institute, Accessed 1 Dec 2015. https://blogs.cfainstitute.org/investor/2015/08/18/the-importance-of-meditation-forinvestment-professionals/

Saft, James. 2013. Meditation and the Art of Investment. *Reuters*. http://blogs.reuters.com/james-saft/2013/04/17/meditation-and-the-art-of-investment/

Sheng Yen. 2019. *108 Wisdom Words by Ven. Sheng Yen*. Dharma Drum Mountain Atlanta. Accessed 28 Aug 2019. https://www.ddmbaatlanta.com/108wisdom-en

Thich, Nhat Hanh. 1988. The Individual, Society, and Nature. In *The Path of Compassion: Writings on Socially Engaged Buddhism*, ed. Fred Eppsteiner. Berkeley: Parallax Press.

———. 2010. *Exclusive Interview with Oprah*. Plum Village. Last modified 28 May 2010. https://plumvillage.org/thich-nhat-hanh-interviews/oprah-talks-to-thich-nhat-hanh/

Welford, Richard. 2007. Examining, Discussing and Suggesting the Possible Contribution and Role of Buddhist Economics for Corporate Social Responsibility. *International Journal of Green Economics* 1 (3/4): 341–350.

Index[1]

A

[1] Note: Page numbers followed by 'n' refer to notes.

E. C. H. Ng, *Introduction to Buddhist Economics*,
Studies in Buddhist Economics, Management, and Policy,
https://doi.org/10.1007/978-3-030-35114-4

The manufacturer's authorised representative in the EU is Springer Nature Customer Service Centre GmbH, Europaplatz 3, 69115 Heidelberg, Germany. If you have any concerns regarding our products, please contact ProductSafety@springernature.com

Printed and bound by CPI Group (UK) Ltd, Croydon, CR0 4YY
30/09/2026
02225442-0006